Please renew/return this item by the last date shown.

So that your telephone call is charged at local rate,
please call the numbers as set out below:

	From Area codes 01923 or 020:	From the rest of Herts:
Renewals:	01923 471373	01438 737373
Enquiries:	01923 471333	01438 737333
Textphone:	01923 471599	01438 737599

L32   www.hertsdirect.org/librarycatalogue

AIRSHIP
PILOT NO.28

T.B. Williams photographed at 7,000 feet in a Balloon Basket in 1915.

AIRSHIP PILOT NO.28

CAPTAIN T.B. WILLIAMS, AFC

With a foreword by
LORD VENTRY

WILLIAM KIMBER · LONDON

First published in 1974 by
WILLIAM KIMBER & CO. LIMITED
Godolphin House, 22a Queen Anne's Gate,
London SW1H 9AE

Typeset by
Specialised Offset Services Ltd., Liverpool
and printed in Great Britain by
Robert MacLehose and Co. Ltd.,
The University Press, Glasgow.

Contents

List of Illustrations

For my wife,
who hopes that I have now
got it out of my system

Foreword

by The Right Honourable The Lord Ventry

Captain Williams and I first met at Pulham, and we have been good friends ever since, so it is an honour to have been asked to attempt an introduction to this book.

Many books have been written about airships, but very few by airship pilots. This is among the first to be written by a British airship pilot recounting his own experiences. It gives a vivid account of what actually occurred on a patrol station, so perhaps a little of the background may be useful.

Up to just before August 1914 all our Service airships were based at Farnborough. They gained little publicity except when there was a mishap. The number of times some of the airships, like *Beta*, were said to be wrecked is extraordinary. Until November, 1918, little was ever written about the Royal Naval Airship Service. There were no glamour boys in that Service, but how keen the vast majority were and how they lived for their 'ships.

Brigadier General E.M. Maitland, soon to die in *R-38*, was Superintendent of Airships, and what an inspiration he was. He was indeed a leader of men.

In August 1914 there were six airships capable of being flown, but the Astra Torres No.3, and Parseval No.4, were the only ones of operational value. These performed yeoman service by patrolling the Straits of Dover for long hours when the original British Expeditionary Force was crossing to France.

In November 1918 there were 103 airships in use. In August 1914 Farnborough with two small sheds, and Kingsnorth with much bigger sheds, but still uncompleted, were the only Service airship stations. By the end of the war there were 18 with others under construction and projected, and there were about a dozen mooring out stations in addition. Likewise personnel grew from 194 officers and men to 7,114. The 216 airships had flown 88,717 hours and covered 2,245,810 miles.

Except for those employed with airships there were few who believed in them and in February 1915 the then First Lord, the late Winston Churchill, wanted to cut the Airship Service right down to the bone, with bases at Barrow and Kingsnorth housing a couple of Astra Torres ships, Nos. 3 and 8 and Parsevals 4, 6 and 7 and personnel to be cut down to man just these ships.

But in the same month the U-boat campaign began and the First Sea Lord, the late Lord Fisher, called into being a fleet of small airships to patrol the narrow seas against the U-boats and guard shipping. There was a conference at the Admiralty on 28th February 1915 and orders were given to produce the first Submarine Scout airship. This ship was up for the first time on 18th March at Kingsnorth, and on the same day 12 more were ordered. Junior officers were brought in from the Grand Fleet and direct entry civilians also, and that is how the writer of this book began his association with airships.

The first of the new bases was put up at Capel near Dover, and by the summer of 1915 sheds were ready at Polegate near Eastbourne, Anglesey, and Luce Bay. A glance at a map will show why these places were decided on. They dominated the eastern entrance and exit to the English Channel and guarded the narrow channel between Larne and Stranraer, and between Holyhead and Dublin.

While the SS airships were patrolling the Narrow Seas in 1916 the larger twin-engined Coastal of 'C' Class airships were commissioned. To guard the South Western Approaches a station was built at Mullion, while the base at Pembroke helped to protect the southern entrance to the Irish Sea.

To work with the Grand Fleet and harry U-boats attacking East Coast traffic, bases were erected at Longside near Peterhead and East Fortune near Edinburgh, with another large base at Howden on the Humber and at Pulham in Norfolk. At all these stations there were great sheds for the rigid airships of the future. Barrow

and Kingsnorth became constructional stations in 1915 and
Wormwood Scrubs concentrated on erecting SS ships from 1917
onwards. In addition there were the rigid constructional stations at
Barlow, Cardington and Inchinnan.

In 1917 the handy SS Zeros were commissioned and in 1918
the twin engined SS ships known as Twins. The North Sea Class
were also produced. These carried double crews, insulated from
the noise and vibration, and flights up to 100 hours were carried
out. After their initial teething troubles, the North Sea Ships were
the finest non-rigid airships of their day and made up for the lack
of efficient rigid airships which the late Air Commodore E.A.
Masterman, then a Wing Captain, was working so hard to bring
into being. He was the first Britisher ever to pilot a rigid airship
and led the Airship Service until the summer of 1915. He, like
Maitland, was a fine leader of men and a great organizer. In charge
of the design, construction and testing of non-rigid airships was
the late Wing Commander T.R. Cave-Browne-Cave. His staff
produced the craft which the author of this book actually piloted.
Having carried out most of his operational flying from Anglesey
our author finished the war at Pulham where he and I first met in
that wonderful summer of 1921 when *R-33* and *R-36* were
proving the value of the Scott mooring mast. This introduction
began with a memory of Pulham and there it ends. So 'Hands off',
as the airship pilot would say, and let the author begin.

Introduction

Over forty years have passed since *R-101*, the last of the British airships, was lost, and with it so many of the pioneers of the airship world.

It is true that Lord Ventry built the *Bournemouth* a small non-rigid in 1951; a wonderful gesture; a great act of faith, but lamentably producing little public interest. The hopes of those who had become fascinated with the prospect of great liners of the air were sadly dashed, and the few were left to mourn the absence of the many with whom they had flown.

There are several records of lighter-than-air craft, as airships are called, and accounts of outstanding flights, but seldom will be found any record of the work of an airship pilot during the war of 1914-1918. I venture to suggest that the value of the small airships during this period was of immense importance to the country, out of all proportion to the number of men and amount of material employed, and that it is high time that this should be appreciated. There was nothing in existence then that could carry out the work performed by the non-rigid airship.

No ship on the sea was lost when being escorted by these airships, when travelling either in or out of convoy. No heavier-than-air craft at this time was able to carry out this work of protection.

It is impossible to write such an account without a constant repetition of the world 'I' — no statement of an individual's experiences can be given without doing so — but I have tried to be objective and to paint the picture as I saw it. I have drawn on accounts from my log books and reports, written at the time, of the training of an airship pilot; the patrolling of the trade routes and escorting of the great convoys coming from the Atlantic into port. This work was carried out by the non-rigid airships, mostly of small size, as the large rigids were not sufficiently developed to carry out these operations; indeed, it would not have been economical to have employed them in this way.

The story of the first aircraft flight from Italy to England, carried out by a British crew flying an Italian semi-rigid airship bought by Britain, is told from first hand.

Post-war developments are related, in many of which I was involved, up to the cessation of airship activities in England.

Finally, there is a review of later opinions on, and interest in, the future of airships, and their great potentialities.

The appendices are full of figures, which can be easily avoided by those who do not like them.

I acknowledge with very grateful thanks the assistance received from the writers of other books, which are included in the Bibliography.

Apley House
Trebarwith Crescent
Newquay, Cornwall

Prologue

'But what *is* an airship?' I must admit to being startled by being asked this question by a university graduate with whom I went ballooning in the summer of 1969, until I realized that very few people under the age of forty can have seen an airship in this country until the arrival of the *Europa* the 300th Goodyear airship, so I have tried to answer this question, without too much technicality, to enable a wider circle of readers to follow the details of their construction and operation.

If you look at the illustrations you will see that an airship is more or less cigar-shaped balloons, which shape is called streamlined, that is a form that offers least resistance to the air they are travelling in. The hull overhead is partially filled with a gas, lighter than air, which carries the weight of the whole structure. In the cars slung underneath are the crew; the control car forward if there are more than one and the engine cars in the rear and on each side. The engines only have the task of pushing or pulling the airship through the air, unlike an aeroplane in which the engines also have to lift the structure by means of forward movement.

There are three main varieties of airships: firstly a non-rigid, usually of small size, where the envelope, as the great gasbag is called, is not re-inforced except at the nose and it keeps its shape by the gas pressure inside; secondly, a semi-rigid, which is similar but the retention of shape is assisted by the attachment of a girder-work keel under the envelope from end to end; the third type is the great rigid. This must be sufficiently large to have enough gas capacity to lift the girder-work framing inside the outer cover of the envelope and in addition the normal control-car and engine nacelles, which are attached to the girder work by rigging.

Cables running from the control cars operate elevators and rudders in the tail which steer the airship up and down and to the left and right. If the engine or engines of an airship stop, the vessel behaves as a free balloon, so every airship pilot must first have an aeronaut's training.

As an airship rises the depth of atmosphere above it decreases: the pressure decreases accordingly and the gas in the envelope expands. Conversely, as an airship descends the depth of atmosphere above it increases: the pressure increases and the gas contracts.

It will be realized that as the shape of a non-rigid and semi-rigid is kept up by the gas pressure, some method must be adopted to adjust the pressure when the airship is going up or coming down. This is effected by fitting air bags called ballonets inside the envelope, usually one forward and another aft, from which air is valved out when climbing or pumped in when descending. A convenient method of doing the latter is by trapping the slipstream of air from the propeller, or airscrew as it is sometimes called. The air is forced up the large piping between the engine and envelope which is a prominent feature of non-rigid and semi-rigid airships.

The rigid's shape being dependent on its girder-construction does not need air ballonets, it has a number of gasbags like cheeses on their sides and the gas inside can expand or contract, within the range of the bag's capacity, in accordance with changes in atmospheric pressure. When rising, if such a height is reached that one or more gasbags are full, any increase in height means that gas has to be discharged either by automatic or manual valves, otherwise the bag or bags would burst. The expansion or contraction of the gas is also affected by temperature. On a hot sunny day the gas will expand. At night or in cold weather the gas will contract. In each case the lift will be affected accordingly.

The non-rigid airships had open control cars, with little protection from the elements. During the 1914-1918 war, the crew were exposed to the weather during many flights of long duration while patrolling shipping routes, or escorting convoys, so thick flying clothes were essential, particularly in winter.

In the small airships, like the SSs, the pilots were sitting in their little bucket seats for many hours on end working with hands and feet to keep their airship on its course and height.

Like other technical jobs, the airship pilot's training is a long and arduous one. First of all he must be trained in ballooning because, as I have pointed out, the airship becomes a balloon if the engine fails. Free ballooning — that is with an untethered spherical balloon — is quite fascinating. The balloon, basket for the pilot and passengers, and equipment comprising trail rope, grapnel and a hoop to which rigging is attached to connect the balloon with the basket, are taken to a supply of gas, either coal gas or hydrogen. The balloon is laid out in a circle, with a net covering it and sandbags hooked on to the perimeter in the meshes of the net. A flexible hose carries the gas from the container to the balloon through a neck, which is tied off by a cord when sufficient gas has been taken in, but opened when the balloon is ready to leave the ground, so that as the balloon rises expanding gas can escape if the gas-bag becomes full. As the balloon fills with gas through the hose, the sandbags are lowered on the net to allow the gasbag to rise and additional sandbags added to counteract the added lift of the gas that is entering. In time the balloon covered by the net rises sufficiently to allow the rigging hoop attached to the basket, to be toggled onto the net. Sandbags are slung on and piled into the basket to keep it on the ground until the pilot and passengers enter.

Instruments are attached to the rigging to indicate the height; whether the balloon is rising, falling or stationary; and the direction of travel. The pilot and passengers enter the basket. Sand from the bags is gently discharged and the balloon ascends.

There is no covering to the basket so the occupants are open to the elements. As the balloon moves with the body of air there is no lateral wind. Air movement is more noticeable as the balloon rises or falls.

Landing a balloon is the most difficult part. When the basket in which the crew is being carried reaches the ground it is travelling at the speed of the wind, and is often thrown on its side and dragged along. It is quite an art to pick a soft spot on which to land and to avoid being thrown out.

When a landing is planned, a long rope is lowered, called the trail rope. This is literally trailed across country and acts as a balancing medium. If the balloon descends there is more weight of rope on the ground and less on the balloon so it will rise, and vice versa. These movements tend to keep the balloon at an average even height above the ground. Care should be taken to lift the end of the trail-rope off the ground when obstacles are reached, to avoid doing damage. People on the ground should be discouraged from catching hold of the rope in a wind, in the vain hope that they are going to be able to hold the moving balloon.

On one occasion I remember a farm labourer jumped onto the tip of our tail-rope with both feet with this idea in view. To his astonishment he was flipped up into the air and stood on his head. Fortunately he was quite unhurt.

When a landing is decided upon and the earth comes closer, a grapnel is slid down the trail rope which hooks onto say, a hedge, and at the same time a rip panel is opened in the gas bag above. The gas then escapes, and the gas bag and basket are spread out tidily on the ground — you hope!

In the revival now taking place in the use of hot air balloons, which in 1783 were the first type of aircraft ever to fly, the lift is obtained by heating the air inside an inflated balloon by means of a propane gas burner. The air inside the balloon becomes lighter because of its being heated and therefore rises, reaching a point when it is capable of lifting a balloon with its basket and contents. If the burner is not used the air inside the balloon cools and allows it to sink to the ground. No sand for ballasting therefore has to be carried, but propane gas in a liquid form in cylinders instead.

In flying an airship, it must be remembered that it behaves like a balloon until engine power is used; excepting that its shape and its elevator and rudder surfaces render it essential to keep the bow into the wind, when being handled by the landing party, or by some mechanical means, on the ground. The airship on the ground is controlled by guy-ropes attached near the bows, with handling assistance on stern-guys, and on the control car.

The buoyancy is tested before leaving the shed and weight removed so that a condition is reached when the ship is just 'light', that is, it would slowly rise if not restrained. The airship is then 'walked' or towed onto the landing ground, lift and trim tested and the engines started.

When conditions are satisfactory the order is given to 'let go'.

The airship then gently rises from the ground into the wind while the engines are accelerated and the pilot or coxswain controls the movements of the ship by steering and elevating wheels. In the case of the small SS non-rigids, all the work is done by the pilot, who steers with his feet while his hands are occupied with engine and ballonet controls. When airborne the airship is put on its course.

When landing, the buoyancy is determined and the airship comes down nose to wind to a landing party, or a mechanical handling device, and is secured.

Considerable research was done into methods of mooring airships in the open, particularly with fixed mooring masts which were used by the rigids to some extent up to the cessation of airship flying. I was in charge of the Pulham Mooring Mast for some time and later collated details of airship mooring systems for Air Ministry records.

Hydrogen gas was used in all the British, French, German and Italian airships. Helium, a non-inflammable gas, separated from natural gas, was used by the later American airships.

Chapter 1

Men Take to the Air

The classical myth of flying is that of Daedalus and Icarus, who were supposed to have escaped from Crete with home-made wings, though Icarus perished in the effort.

There were many attempts in history for men to fly in this fashion, most of them being fatal, until it was realized that man's muscles were not designed by nature for flapping wings. But the desire to imitate the birds was deeply rooted and at last, with the assistance of balloons, man was able to get off the ground.

There were many designs for 'flying ships' and in Paris on 21st November, 1783 Pilatre de Rozier and the Marquis d'Arlandes made the first ascent in a Montgolfier hot air balloon. In the same year, on 1st December, also in Paris, J.A.C. Charles made an ascent in a hydrogen balloon; while Jeffries and Blanchard made an ascent in London in 1784. The latter pair made the first Channel crossing by air in 1785.

In 1794 tethered balloons, the forerunner of the Kite balloon, were first used for military observation by the French Army at Mauberge. Several parachute landings from balloons were carried out by A.J. Garnerin over Paris in 1797.

Great efforts were now made to design a balloon that could be driven along and it was realized that elongation of the gasbag would be of assistance. The absence of a suitable engine, however, held up progress.

In the meantime a record flight of 480 miles was made in a balloon from London to Weilberg in Germany in 1836. Tethered balloons were used in the American Civil war by the Federal Army during 1861-1865. In 1870 during the Franco-Prussion war, fifty-eight successful flights in free balloons were made, carrying people and despatches.

As far as airships were concerned we must credit Henri Giffard with the first flight in 1852, but his airship which was powered by a steam engine could only fly at 5 miles per hour. Later Paul Haenlin constructed an airship with an engine burning coal gas drawn from the envelope. By 1888 the internal combustion engine was invented and within a few years applied to the traction of vehicles on land and in the air.

Zeppelin No.1 flew in 1900 and in 1901 Santos Dumont flew his airship No.VI round the Eiffel Tower. To quote Santos Dumont's own report: 'The airship carried by the impetus of its great speed, passed on as a racehorse passes the winning post, as a sailing yacht passes the winning line, as a road racing automobile continues flying past the judges who have snapped its time'. His speed was about 14 miles per hour.

1903 saw the first flight of a powered aeroplane by Orville Wright in the United States. In England, Army dirigible No.1 — a dirigible means a steerable balloon — the *Nulli Secundus* was flying in 1907 and the Spencer Brothers' dirigible in 1908; the *Baby* was flying in 1909 and passed on its envelope to the *Beta* in the following year, when the *Gamma* was completed and the *Delta* commenced. All British airships had so far been non-rigids with the exception of a small rigid *R-1* which was built and ominously called the *Mayfly*. It was completed in 1911 and wrecked during trials. The *Delta*, completed about the same time, was intended to be a semi-rigid but was altered into a non-rigid.

As Continental countries were tending to get ahead of us in airship development, a Clement-Bayard was acquired from France in 1910 and based at Wormwood Scrubs. This proved very unsatisfactory and was deflated. A Lebaudy was also purchased about the same time. This was subscribed for by readers of the *Morning Post* and flew from Paris to London. It had two Panhard-Levassor engines of 150 horsepower and flew at about 30 miles per hour. A shed was built at Farnborough to take it. The height of the airship was increased during manufacture without

Farnborough being informed, strange though it may seem, and the ship was ripped from end to end as she was being docked. She was rebuilt and the height of the shed increased, but on trial she collided with a house, never to fly again!

In 1913 a Parseval non-rigid was obtained from Germany, known as No.4; with two duplicates built by Vickers Ltd – Nos. 6 and 7 – she carried out very useful training work, and some escorting of the British Expeditionary Force in 1914. An Astra-Torres was also bought from France, known as No.8. This airship was the forerunner of our Coastal and North Sea Classes which were non-rigids with a system of internal rigging.

There were great pioneers of British airship flying, as in heavier-than-air craft. Names that spring to the mind are those of men such as Colonel Capper who held Airship Certificate No.1 and Lieutenant Commander Pollock who held Aeronauts' Certificate No. 1 and taught us our ballooning. I was privileged to act as assistant balloon instructor to C.F. Pollock for a short period during the 1914-1918 war, in the intervals of delivering new airships to active service stations, and learned to respect his patience and good judgment. He was a genius at judging the alteration in wind direction at various heights, and often named the very area we would reach on a balloon journey. The number of times we had tea in a great country house was not as coincidental as it appeared – and there would always be a horse and cart available to take our balloon, neatly packed in its basket, to the nearest railway station for its return to Hurlingham.

Pollock made his first crossing of the English Channel by balloon from Eastbourne in 1899 and by 1910 had crossed eleven times. He was a kindly man, ever appreciative of service given to him. On one occasion, I remember, when he wished to repay the kindness of our hosts in giving us landing facilities, we were able to give several children a short lift off the ground and down again, much to their delight. We were very distressed to hear later that he had been struck down with an incurable and progressive paralysis.

Colonel Capper, who had built Army Dirigible No.1, the *Nulli Secundus*, was accompanied by C.M. Waterlow and S.F. Cody when he flew her to London late in 1909 from Farnborough, sailing grandly round St Paul's Cathedral at 18 miles an hour. Unfortunately the wind became too strong for them to return, but they were able to land on the cycle track at the Crystal Palace. There they deflated, packed up and returned to base by horse and cart. Capper had Airship Pilot's Certificate No.1, while Waterlow, who flew with him, had No.3, both of the same date: 14th February 1911. Waterlow was an instructor in airship techniques in the 1914-1918 war. Several times in lectures I have heard him say: 'If you are in a landing party and get carried off your feet, let go at once'. On the 25th July, 1917, with the airship *SS-39* at Cranwell, he found himself in just this position — but he failed to let go in time and was killed.

By 1914, France had developed her own type of non-rigid airships, while Italy specialized in semi-rigids. Germany, under the driving power of Count Zeppelin, kept to the large rigids. Since 1900 when the first Zeppelin had flown from a floating balloon shed on Lake Constance, *LZ-2* had flown in January 1906, followed by *LZ-4* in 1908. In the following year, 1909, Count Zeppelin was joined by Dr. Hugo Eckener, one of the greatest airship pilots of all time, who later established the world's first passenger airship service. On 4th March, 1912, a small Zeppelin called the *Viktoria Luise* carried 23 passengers a distance of 200 miles in under 8 hours. This airship had flown about 400 journeys by the end of 1913. By August 1914, the *Viktoria Luise, Sachsen* and *Hansa* had covered over 65,000 miles and carried over 19,000 passengers.

Between 1900 and 1914 twenty-four Zeppelins were built, and ten of the most modern of these were available for Germany at the outbreak of war in 1914.

In Great Britain, the Royal Flying Corps had been created on the 13th May, 1912 to cover all air activities; on the 1st July 1914, the Royal Naval Air Service was formed, taking to itself all naval air interests, including airships.

Soon after the outbreak of war in 1914 the Navy bought a small non-rigid airship from E.T. Willows which had a promising

Left: Squadron Leader
C.F. Pollock on a
Balloon flight in 1916.
He held Aeronaut's
Certificate No.1.

Below: A balloon in
flight over London in
1916 photographed by
T.B. Williams from a
higher Balloon.

The first British Rigid Airship to fly.

performance. It was decided to fit the envelope of this airship with the fuselage of a BE 2c aeroplane, which work was completed in two weeks. The trials proved so satisfactory that a number of ships of this type were ordered, to be known as the SS – Submarine Searcher-Class. Of the 162 built, 29 had the fuselage of a BE 2c aeroplane as a car; 10 were built with a similar fuselage made by Armstrong-Whitworth; 26 had the fuselage of a Maurice Farman aeroplane; 6 had special cars and were the SS-Pushers; 76 were SS Zeros with boat-shaped cars; 12 were SS-Twins; and finally, there were three 'Experimentals'. The gas capacity for the earliest was 60,000 cubic feet, soon increasing to 70,000 while the Twins had a 100,000 cubic feet envelope.

Before the war we had bought an Astra-Torres airship from the French and used this design for the production of a Coastal airship, the first being ready at the end of 1915; 27 of these were built of a capacity of 170,000 cubic feet and another 12 of 200,000 cubic feet called 'C-Stars'. There were 16 larger ships of this type of 360,000 cubic-feet called *North-Sea* designed to work with the Fleet.

After the failure of Rigid Airship No.1 – the *Mayfly*, which broke her back on being floated out of her shed at Barrow – no further work was carried out on a rigid until No.9 was ordered in the middle of 1914, of similar construction to a Zeppelin. Her design was prepared by Vickers Limited. This ship did some trial work and was deflated in 1918. Excluding the *Mayfly*, we built 16 rigid airships: No.9, Numbers 23 to 25 inclusive; *R-26*, *R-27*, and *R-29*, all of parallel shape; *R-31* and *R-32* of Schutte-Lanz wooden-type construction and stream-lined shape; *R-33* and *R-34*, with which a considerable amount of mooring-mast trials were carried out; *R-36*, fitted for passenger carrying; *R-38* which was sold to the Americans, but was lost on her trials; *R-80*, a small edition of *R-33* and used for training; and finally *R-100* and *R-101*. The *R-34* carried out a double crossing of the Atlantic, the first aircraft to do so, as will be described later.

However, it was the non-rigids, particularly the SSs, which were the most useful and these airships — which proved of such great value on escort work during World War One — take up a large part of this book.

If you want to know what SS means I regret to say that I don't know. It is said that Lord Fisher, the First Sea Lord, demanded on 28th February 1915 submarine-searching airships, but some others call them submarine-scouts. Official text books seem to dodge the issue by sticking to SS. Make your own choice.

In addition to the rigid and non-rigid airships detailed above, a semi-rigid was purchased from the Italian Government by the British Government and in the summer of 1918 a crew, of which I was Chief Officer, left for Rome to fly the airship back to England. The Captain was George Meager.

Chapter 2

Early Days

As a boy I was thrilled by accounts of the early efforts of men to fly, and at weekends I would travel out to Hendon from Hampstead and then, in a field, I would watch adventurous men, with their caps on back to front, sitting in little seats, surrounded by fabric, string, wire and struts which were the rudimentary aeroplanes of that time.

There were great occasions when one or other of the crazy craft actually got off the ground. Geoffrey de Havilland, relates in his book *Sky Fever** that in 1910 Frank Hearle, his engineer, was able to tell him that he was 'several inches off the ground for about twenty yards'. (Later between the two Great Wars, I was fated to spend fourteen years of my life with the de Havilland organization.) Before long Graham White had managed to cover half a mile at a height of 30 to 40 feet.

In 1906 the *Daily Mail* had offered a prize of ten thousand pounds for the first flight from Hendon to Manchester. An evening paper, *The Star*, offered ten million pounds, and added 'one offer is as safe as the other'; *Punch* offered a prize for the first man to swim the Atlantic. And then in 1910 Louis Paulhan won the *Daily Mail* prize; presumably by then the *Star*'s offer had been withdrawn. I was quite fascinated by these happenings and was rewarded by being allowed sometimes to help at Hendon. I would go home covered in grease and filling the air with the aroma of Castrol, but as happy as pie.

The year 1909 was a landmark for the aeroplane. Bleriot flew the English Channel; the first British Air Meeting was held at Blackpool and the first International Air Meeting at Rheims.

* Published by Hamish Hamilton in 1961.

In 1910 the Secretary of State for War stated that he could not see any use for aircraft in war. The Cavalry objected to aircraft because they might frighten the horses.

When the war broke out in 1914, as a junior in the managerial department of a large shipping company, I was given my turn at sitting all night by a telephone in the Board Room to listen for calls in connection with casualties in the Company's fleet. It nearly drove me mad. I would sit there in the quiet of the night, while there was action outside – possibly air action – and here was I imprisoned, waiting for the telephone to ring. At last I went to my father and said that I felt that I was not doing my share. He at first tried to persuade me that I was doing a useful job. Later, on my insistence, he asked me what I wanted to do. A psychologist friend had told me that I would make a good military aviator. I was not quite sure what that meant, but repeated it to my father.

'Explain yourself', said he.

'I want to fly', I said simply.

'Fly?' said the old man. 'If the Maker intended men to fly he would have given them wings'! – Which remark was probably not original.

However, I persisted and persisted, and Father, who was a retired Lieutenant in the Royal Naval Reserve, took me to a friend of his at the Admiralty. The old Admiral listened to my father's story. Then he said to me: 'We are going to build some airships. They will be Naval ships of war, wearing the white ensign. Would you like to fly one?'

I almost swooned with excitement as I answered: 'Yes, sir'!

Soon I was summoned to attend an interviewing board of awe-inspiring Naval Officers with much gold braid, penetrating eyes and enquiring tongues. Later I was ordered to the Royal Naval College at Greenwich and examined medically, physically and mentally.

Then one wonderful morning at the end of 1915 my mother passed to me at breakfast time a large OHMS envelope addressed to Probationary Flight Sub Lieutenant T.B. Williams, RN. What this meant to me was indescribable: I was in!

My appointment was to HMS *President*, a 'mother-ship' lying in the Thames, but I had to report to a naval airship station establishment on Wormwood Scrubs Common, to the west of London. I presented myself with much trepidation to the Commanding Officer, Lieutenant Commander Corbett-Wilson.

He received me very kindly and put me to work assisting the Duty Officer of the day and gave me some preliminary instruction. On that day I found that I had committed my first boob as a budding Naval Officer. My father was away at the time or I am sure that it would not have happened. I had dressed myself very carefully and nattily in my lovely navy blue uniform, built by a great London outfitter, and had no difficulty in carrying the weight of gold braid on my sleeves. I had however fitted myself up with a navy blue tie instead of a black one. This scandalous disrespect for Lord Nelson was the talk of my little corner of the Royal Navy for some time!

My father died in 1916 at which time he was Secretary of the Mercantile Marine Service Association. He had by then accepted me proudly as a naval officer, but still viewed the birds on my sleeves with some reserve.

Early days at Wormwood Scrubs were taken up with drill, lectures and study. I remember the excellent instruction in knots, splicing and rigging, and I still tie bowlines, sheet-bends and reef-knots as a habit. A Warrant Officer took us into the mysteries of eta-patches, valves, sleeves, petticoats, crabpots, fabric, and ballonets. We had to take our turns by day and night as Duty Officer and discipline was pumped into us.

At long last several of us were loaded into a lorry and taken to Hurlingham Polo Ground to commence our balloon course. My *Pilot's Flying Log book* reminds me that we attended at Hurlingham on 18th January, 1916, three days after my birthday, and received our first practical instruction in laying out and filling a gas-bag, with coal gas from the local gas works. The gas bag on this occasion was the balloon *Swallow*. I haven't a record of its capacity, but it was probably 60,000 cubic feet. The instructor was Warrant Officer King, and the passengers — four young probationary Flight Sub Lieutenants, one named Williams. So we followed in the footsteps of de Rozier and d'Arlandes, the world's first balloonists in 1783.

The *Swallow* left the polo ground at Hurlingham on an east-north-east course which took her over London. As a free balloon has no engine, it must travel with the wind. My log states that we passed near St Paul's Cathedral at a height of 1,200 feet. We went easterly over Hackney Marshes and landed at Collier's Row, near Romford.

Five days later we travelled in the balloon *Shrimp* to Mildenhall in Suffolk, via Hyde Park; Lieutenant Commander C.F. Pollock was our Instructor. One of the pupils had to be reprimanded for trying to bomb a bus with currant buns at Marble Arch. Next day in the *Salmon* we landed at Boughton. Four days later in the *Seahorse* we ran into thick fog and landed at Chingford.

On 1st February was my own pass out and solo in the balloon *Plover* of 60,000 cubic feet. We left Hurlingham at midday making due west; passed over Roehampton Kite-balloon Station 10 minutes later and crossed the river near Richmond. I landed my instructor, Petty Officer Ford and passengers at Staines Reservoir at 2.27 p.m. and set off alone on my solo trip. Suddenly a thunderstorm broke out and I went up like a rocket, not stopping until I had reached 13,000 feet, a considerable height above several layers of clouds. It was very quiet and cold and lonely.

I brought the *Plover* down as gently as I could, seeming to go 'plop' as I re-entered the upper cloud strata, reaching equilibrium under several cloud layers at 1,000 feet from the ground. I then brought the balloon down, put out the trail rope, and shouted to some farm workers, asking the name of the place. They nearly jumped out of their skins. They however shouted a reply which I had difficulty in hearing, but picked out the Fox Hills on my map as most likely. I found later that they had been shouting 'Pirbright'. A large town was approaching me, or rather I was approaching it, so I decided to land in a field beside the railway line which proved to be Ashvale near Aldershot.

Airship Pilot's Certificate No. 28 issued to T. B. Williams in May 1917.

I remember being rather proud of my landing at the time. It wasn't easy for a novice. There was a long field, with the railway, many telegraph lines, and a canal in my track, but I got my grapnel down and pulled out the ripping panel in accordance with the copy book and it all worked, to my great relief, as I only just fitted into the field I had selected. I eased my bump in the basket by dropping the contents of a sandbag out at a late moment. Instead of fine sand it was lumps of earth taken in at Staines Reservoir which fell in great clods one of which struck a large galvanized bath tub hanging on the outside wall of a cottage; it chopped the bath off the wall like cheese. The noise was appalling and an old lady peering through the door disappeared inside as though the devil was after her!

I received ample assistance from the Aircraft Experimental Station at Farnborough in packing and transport to Aldershot railway station. I had been 4 hours 13 minutes on my flight.

It was not until the 20th April that I was able to carry out my balloon night flight. This was in the *North Star*, 80,000 cubic feet, flying from Reading to Langley, to the west of Windsor, and it qualified me for my Aeronaut's Certificate No.78 dated 8th May, 1916.

There is nothing at all like free-ballooning. The impression is that the earth leaves you and passes to one side as you ask for 'Hands off, let go' from the handling party. Like a great map are spread the fields, rivers and towns, which get smaller as you gaze. You are in the body of air and therefore have no movement of your own. It is only on rising or falling, in or out of clouds, that you meet any local landmarks in your world of peace. There is no wind because you are travelling with it.

On a clear day the great gas bag above you is set in a sky indescribably blue with the sun showing every wrinkle and knot of the netting. From its open lower end hangs the white valve cord and the red rip cord. The long suspension lines from the net are attached to the square basket, which creaks as the crew move about.

As you rise the sounds, one by one, slowly disappear, to complete the silence and serenity.

During our early training at Wormwood Scrubs we had been given a small hydrogen balloon made of gold beaters' skin that would just lift a man to a limited height. It was let up on a winch and had to lift an ever increasing weight of wire as the balloon ascended, so the height depended on the weight of the man. The wire was attached to a short length of planking, like a bosun's chair, slung under the gas bag, the latter being filled with hydrogen. The young pilots in training were let up on this contraption in turn to give them 'air sense' and were seated on the piece of wood with their legs dangling. I know of more pleasant

B

situations, but we had of course to appear nonchalant. There was an officer very slightly senior to us who used to march us off to drill. He started to do the heavy and throw his weight about unduly, which was much resented. One day we had him up on the plank and pretended to forget him and started to walk away. He shouted madly and tried to pull himself down. Eventually we relented and brought him down by the winch, apologizing profusely. I, being about the lightest, went up the highest, so I had to mind my p's and q's.

On the 21st February we heard that Wing Commander Neville Usborn, RN, who had been appointed on 13th August 1915 as 'Inspecting Commander of Airships (Building)' with an aeroplane pilot named Ireland, had taken up an aeroplane attached to an airship gasbag at Kingsnorth, Chatham. It was the first experiment of this kind. They had fittings made to their own design, but the rear attachment failed to operate and they were killed.

At last towards the end of February 1916 a small non-rigid airship SS-36 fitted with a Maurice Farman aeroplane fuselage as a control car, arrived at Wormwood Scrubs to be used for training purposes; the engine was a 75 hp air-cooled Renault of the pusher type. There was intense competition amongst us to get some flying instruction in her.

On the 28th I had a 12-minute flight with Flight Lieutenant Wood, taking off over the exercise yard of Wormwood Scrubs Prison, which became quite familiar. We could see the prisoners walking round the exercise yard. On my fifth flight I was allowed to take over the controls in the air and on the 1st April piloted her for a complete flight.

I took the opportunity of a trip in a tethered 'S' type kite balloon on the 16th May. Three of us went up to 2,000 feet in a small basket. The balloon had a horrible trick of doing spiral nose-dives without warning, which was very unpleasant, as there was no warning, no parachutes and little faith in the belief that the balloon would recover!

On the 12th May I was acting as navigator in a BE 2c aeroplane on a short journey between Wormwood Scrubs and Hendon. I had very little notice of the trip and borrowed a flying helmet just as I got into the machine. The helmet was much too big for me, but better than nothing in the very open cockpit I had to occupy in front of the pilot, who was an Australian named Ellis.

Very soon I shouted to him: 'Hendon ahead' — but he seemed not to understand, so I rose in my seat as far as my harness would permit and pointed below. At that moment the slipstream of the propeller caught the edge of my helmet and spun it round back to front. I was obliterated — and the pilot laughed so much he almost stalled the aeroplane.

Chapter 3

Kingsnorth

Early in June 1916 I was transferred to the new airship station at Kingsnorth near Chatham where intensive training was being given to the small band of budding airship officers, in both theory and practice, including gunnery and much drill. The long days were filled with lectures on aeronautics, navigation, engineering and meteorology, interspersed with the practical work of flying, rigging, and engine overhaul.

Graduation examinations were held at Kingsnorth following our training, I, in my keeness, attended all the lectures possible and read up everything I could get my hands on, in connection with our work. This resulted in my being called a 'swot' and becoming thoroughly unpopular amongst my contemporaries. I didn't care very much. I wanted to fly and I had learned by experience that one has to work for anything desired. I had nothing to complain about over my position in the examination list.

Our training ships at Kingsnorth were *SS-14* with a BE 2c aeroplane fuselage for a car, and *SS-31*, the latter fitted with a Maurice Farman fuselage and a pusher engine in the rear. I did my passing out flight as a service pilot in *SS-14* on the 5th July.

We later had *C 1*, the first of the Coastal Class, a larger type with a specially built car and driven by two Napier Lion engines. She carried a crew of five. There was also *SS 40*, painted a dull black, which disappeared from time to time — she was used for night work over France, dropping men behind the lines.

Considerable training flying was carried out, including night flights. *SS-14* was the favourite with her tractor propeller, although *SS-31* had better visibility. The latter was slower and harder to fly as she had a tendency to travel almost sideways like a crab and to be sluggish in answering the controls.

Soon after our graduation examinations were over the Captain of *SS-31* was posted away to an active service station and the ship sat forlorn for some days while speculation was rife as to who would get the somewhat despised prize.

Imagine my excitement when on the notice board carrying the Orders of the Day appeared my name as the new commander. I was more disliked than ever! I expect that I swaggered a bit. I just didn't care about such remarks as I sat up with my rather ugly craft at night and dusted her with my handkerchief. She was my pride and joy and I cared not if she was somewhat wayward in the air. There was a challenge in her crabwise movements and ungraceful landings. She was my sweetheart for two whole months.

As Kingsnorth was a testing and construction airship station, as well as being used for training, we had some hazardous times trying out innovations. I remember that S.E. Taylor and I took his *SS-14* on a test flight after a water-cooled Curtiss had been fitted in it in replacement for the 75 h.p. air cooled Renault. We took her up to five or six thousand feet and on the way down found that the radiator had developed a leak. We throttled back but the engine seized up. After ballooning a bit and letting the engine cool, Taylor and I took it in turn to get out on the skids and try to start the engine. She just wouldn't have it.

There was a flat calm so we gently settled down beside the churchyard at Hoo, from whence my mother's family had sprung. Possibly there was some interest from the gravestones, but we were very busy and didn't notice. We stopped the leak with chewing gum from a local shop, had a go at the engine again, after filling the radiator at the village pump, and it started up without much fuss. As we had lost gas in ballooning we raised the air pressure in the ballonets from the slipstream of the propeller in the normal way. The lift was now reduced so Taylor flew his ship back to base while I walked home after telephoning the position to Kingsnorth not far away.

Left: a Maurice Farman
Aeroplane Car.

Above: T.B. Williams piloting SS31 – 'The Flying Bedstead' equipped with a
Maurice Farman Car.

Below: Maurice Farman Biplane.

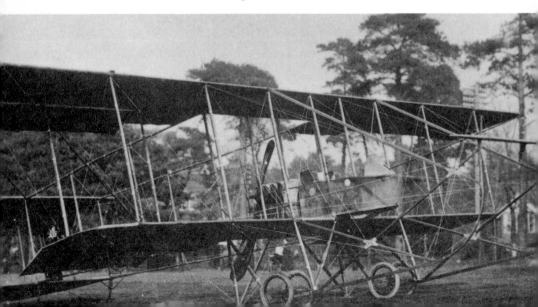

On another occasion I took *SS-14* up with an experimental
rudder on the top of the envelope, instead of underneath, which
was not at all satisfactory. I had considerable difficulty in
returning to the landing ground.

My *SS-31*, now known as 'The Flying Bedstead', was adopted as
the victim for testing any idea, bright or otherwise, emanating
from the back-room boys. My log tells me of several balloon
landings – that is with the airship's engine stopped – which
showed the necessity for the aeronautical instruction. I remember
making a forced landing with *SS-31* at Rainham. Another occasion
was after my long suffering steed had been fitted with a new type
of lacing to the suspensions. I had made a cautious circuit of the
aerodrome when one of the new lacings carried away, releasing my
main starboard suspension which whipped back and broke the
starboard elevator control wire. This in turn cut through my
propeller blades like carrots.

Immediately I heard, or felt, trouble, I slammed my engine
throttle shut. When the series of breakages ceased I found myself
with the car lying over on its starboard side and the starboard
elevator smashed and useless. The engine was ticking over but not
liking it as it was out of balance because of the broken blades.
Fortunately the envelope was not pierced.

S.E. Taylor, the Captain of *SS-14* was with me, as I had been
with him when we had trouble with the new Curtiss engine – I
don't know if he was the Jonah or I. Anyway, we were blessed
with very little wind on this occasion. I sat the ship down as gently
as I could, while half lying on my side, at the cost of a few broken
skid struts. Fortunately, the landing party was very handy and
floated her back to bed.

A new envelope now arrived for *SS-31* and during the process of
re-rigging it was decided to try twin rudders to better the steering,
which had always been erratic. This improved the horizontal
control considerably. I spent the next month giving instructional
flights and completing my training in Coastals.

Occasionally we had visits from aeroplane pilots from East-
church, who would try to show off with their stick and string

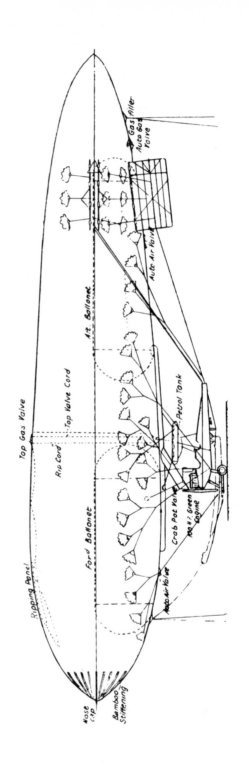

A diagram of an SS airship with a BE2c Car.

contraptions. On one occasion a two-seater got too close to one of our hangar wind-screens which whipped off one of its wings. There resulted a long line on the ground of bits of aeroplane with two slightly injured and very surprised flyers still sitting in their bucket seats, but on the ground.

The aeroplane pilots would say that the airships drifted about like bad smells. We in turn would take them for a ride, then slow down the engine when rising steeply and close to the ground, to hear the agonized cry: 'look out, you'll stall the bloody thing!'

When I could get leave for a day or two I would dash up to London, perhaps for a symphony concert at the Queen's Hall or a theatre, spending the night in my room at the top of my mother's house in Hampstead. I remember travelling in an Underground train late one evening in the autumn and being delayed at a station. Everything was comparatively quiet when my neighbour turned to me and gazed at the gilt bird on the shoulder of my naval greatcoat. In a hoarse alcohol-laden voice he said to me: 'Flying corpse, guv'nor?'

'Not yet', I replied.

I don't think he saw the joke but judging from the roar of laughter, the rest of the passengers did. Perhaps I wouldn't have been so facetious if I could have foreseen the terrible losses of young pilots in the two great wars to follow.

On one occasion I went home with some feverish complaint on me and retired to bed. I had a dreadful nightmare, and dreamed that I was Captain of a great airship, travelling very high and very fast. Everything was working perfectly. From my little seat in the control car I ran my eye over the instruments. All were normal. The officer on watch had just reported after completing his rounds that there was no trouble anywhere. But it was very hot and I didn't like it. I got up from my seat and walked up and down the control car, the Height and Steering Coxswains looking at me enquiringly. I leaned out of the starboard window of the control car and looked at the nacelles with their sweetly running engines, then an upward glance at the great body of the hull.

As I looked I thought I saw a tongue of flame issue from its bulky side. I looked again and was sure: it grew and grew as I watched. I knew that we were using hydrogen as a lifting gas, helium not being available to us, and that there is nothing worse than a hydrogen fire. I raised my hand and gave the signal 'Abandon ship'. My crew numbered twenty-nine and each man was wearing his harness and had a parachute in a rack above him as we were on dangerous work.

The heat became worse and worse as I counted the puffs of parachute silk opening far below. My counting seemed interminable until I reached the twenty-ninth. Then I dropped out upside down into the void while the heat of the flames and the scream of dis-integrating material ended in a great crash — I turned a somersault over the high brass end of my bedstead and broke up my washstand, jug and basin with my head!

My fever was better in the morning.

Occasionally when in London I would attend a Turkish bath establishment. On one of these occasions I got into conversation with a pleasant and intelligent man in one of the cooling rooms. After some talking my companion got to his feet and, eyeing the angle of the wall, gently pressed on it with his hand and then sat down and we talked again. I was very impressed with his knowledge and opinions. He got up again and gently pressed on the opposite wall. On taking his seat once more he said: 'I must ask you to keep my confidence, but I am the Angel Gabriel and my duty is to keep the world on its axis. I can function more efficiently in a Turkish bath'. He was so convincing I almost believed him. A brother airman, perhaps!

It was a relief to be in the hands of one of the attendants who told me the man was well known in all the Turkish baths round London. He did no harm; perhaps some good. Who knows?

Early in my flying career I discovered that doctors dealing with young pilots had laid down that occasional outbursts were essential, to blow off pent emotions. These often gave vent to terrible battles in the Officers' Messes, for no particular reason. They were sometimes organized and sometimes just happened.

One time a polite note arrived in the Gunroom, the junior

One of the sheds at the Royal Naval Airship Station at Kingsnorth. On the left is an SS Airship and the other two are Coastals.

officers' mess, from the seniors in the Wardroom. Would we join them at dinner on a stated date, with some kind of entertainment afterwards? We accepted, even more politely. We arrived well groomed and tried to be 'at ease'.

The Wardroom dined and wined us well and afterwards someone suggested that perhaps some exercise would be suitable, say a wrestling match between the two smallest in the room. The suggestion was received with acclaim. Pullen, one of my messmates and I were selected as suitable material. We removed our natty Number One monkey jackets and carefully hung them over the backs of two chairs. All the winner had to do was to place the loser's shoulders squarely on the floor.

We struggled and pushed and pulled until I decided I would take a rest on the floor, but face downwards. Pullen sat on my back and wore himself out trying to turn me over. Both of us had supporters who were roaring encouragement. I heard a shout: 'Go on Pullen, he's nearly finished' – and Pullen's muttered reply: 'So am I'. This gave me encouragement and I made a great heave, rolled Pullen over, slapped his shoulders on the floor and was proclaimed the winner.

This bout was so much appreciated that, after some further refreshment, it was decided to form teams and what more convenient than Wardroom versus Gunroom?

There was considerable sparring for position to commence with, each man looking for an opponent of about his own weight. At first some kind of rules were observed: Once a gentleman always a gentleman. Soon, however, as casualties occurred, there began a tendency for small groups or individuals to go to the help of their besieged, with no holds barred. An enormous Lieutenant Commander RN (not retired) noticed my light weight and seized me by the ankles and swung me round his head. Tired of knocking down opponents with my poor body he made one more swing and let me go, straight for a window, through which I went, taking the frame with me.

Fortunately we were on the ground floor and I was mercifully received by a large bush growing out of the concrete. I got to my

feet in a towering rage and shook bits of window from my person.
I wasn't going to suffer this indignity. I put my head through the
broken window frame to size up the position only to be grabbed
by the scruff of the neck and thrown across the room. I stayed
where I fell in a corner. I had had enough — and I was not the only
one. Casualties were everywhere and the heat of battle was dying
out.

Two stalwarts were still seeking whom they might devour.
There was a semi-casualty leaning against the swinging doors
leading to the billiard room. The two looked at him; he had no
right to be on his feet; so they seized the piano and pushed it at
him.

The piano slid on its wheels, hit the man and stopped at the
swing doors, but he travelled on to seek his rest on the billiard
table and the doors quietly closed!

I sneaked off to my cabin and so to bed.

The period at Kingsnorth had been on the whole a happy one.
We were near Chatham and sometimes could get in for a break in
the evening if duties permitted; perhaps to an entertainment such
as a hilarious music-hall called, I think, Barnards. The officers were
perched in boxes round the walls with other ranks on the lower
deck below. Chatham having a Naval dockyard was always well
populated with sailors, and the girls were very tough. The Airship
Station was run like a ship and leaving it was called 'going ashore
in the liberty boat'.

At the beginning of November 1916 I was ordered to the Royal
Naval Airship Station at Anglesey, where the airships were
responsible for the escort of the Atlantic convoys coming through
the Irish Sea into Liverpool.

Chapter 4

The War Front at Anglesey

If you study a map of the British Isles you will see that merchant ships crossing the Atlantic and using the Western Approaches into Liverpool, which in World War I was the back door of England, must travel either to the north or south of Ireland -- by either the North Channel or St George's Channel into the Irish Sea.

Airship stations were therefore sited at Stranraer, Luce Bay, on the south-western tip of Scotland; at Anglesey in the centre; at Pembroke in South Wales; and at Mullion in Cornwall. There was an airship building station at Barrow-in-Furness which was very useful in emergency and which I sometimes used when collecting new airships at a later date. Many convoys of merchant ships were brought into British waters escorted by airships; they were usually led by a cruiser with destroyers to port, starboard and astern. The convoys were met by airships, usually SSs, and passed on to Anglesey which station was responsible for the passage through the Irish Sea to Liverpool.

Rear Admiral Murray Sueter, the Royal Navy's senior airman from 1909 to 1917, stated in his book *Airmen or Noahs*, that no merchant ships were lost when escorted by SS or Coastal airships patrolling overhead. He claims that the lack of airships in the Mediterranean cost £2,000,000 per day! It is certain that no aeroplanes were capable of carrying out the work at that time. This was proved by the loss of a flight of six DH 4s sent to assist us in November 1917, when only one of the aeroplanes reached us from the Midlands and the pilot was killed in landing.

Aeroplanes had neither the endurance of the airships nor the ability to fly slowly, if necessary, at the speed of a seaborne ship. Engine failure in an aeroplane meant that it must land at once. An airship could keep in the air like a balloon, held aloft by its lifting gas. There were numerous instances when I was able to return to my base after engine trouble, which would probably have been fatal to an aeroplane, particularly over the sea, or over rough or mountainous country.

At that time no aeroplane could carry out flights of eight, ten, or more hours, as we did regularly – nor did we need a prepared aerodrome. Flights were possible in all but the very worst weather conditions. Fog did not stop us flying as it still does aeroplanes today. In favourable weather we could land gently into the hands of a few men comprising a landing party. In unfavourable weather we could land by trail rope. Night flying was little more difficult than by day and no elaborate landing lights were needed. I once landed in a flat calm, by the light of matches, and at best we had only a few oil flares to guide us.

I still vividly remember the great thrill it gave me to join a convoy with merchant ships covering the sea in all directions, wallowing in the waves which sometimes swept across their decks, a great warship leading them and destroyers running around like sheepdogs attending the flock. We would be met by a flashing Aldis signal lamp from the warship, giving us the news and directions, and would scout ahead searching for mines, or a feather of water indicating the periscope of a German submarine, or even the track of a torpedo. The submarines would not stay and fight, and even if we did not sink many of them, our presence kept them submerged and enabled the precious cargoes of troops and materials to be brought into Liverpool. I shall always hold as a living memory the joy I felt on the safe fulfilment of the task. One was conscious of a great weight of responsibility until the merchant ships had passed the boom into the River Mersey.

When there were no convoys to escort, the trade routes had to be patrolled and coastal vessels, or perhaps a straggler from a convoy, watched. There was always great excitement on the ships when we flew round them, much waving and caps thrown in the air, and blasts from the ship's siren.

When I arrived in Anglesey the Royal Naval Air Station was

A Coastal non rigid
airship at Kingsnorth in
1916.

A North Sea non rigid
airship; double the size
of the Coastals. It could
operate for days on
end.

At first there were no
proper bomb racks,
and the bombsights
were a couple of wire
nails.

hard-pressed because of the German Submarines attacking the Atlantic convoys. The station was equipped with four airships; three BE tractor SSs, Numbers 22, 24 and 25 and a MF pusher, Number 33. The Commanding Officer was Major George Herbert Scott, who was killed in *R-101* when she made a forced landing at Beauvais much later.

I was given command of *SS-25* carrying out a five-hour patrol on my first flight. Our little airships were in the air on most days, sometimes doing more than one flight a day, and often having to land at night. The take off for dawn patrols or some special early flight was of course during darkness. The irregular hours and nibbled sandwich in the air soon became so much a part of one's everyday life they ceased to be noticed.

There were periods when, short of pilots, I would land exhausted and lie asleep on the floor of the officers' mess until I recovered sufficiently to bath and dress and sit down to a meal prepared by Johnston, or one of our other faithful mess stewards. Johnnie would gently push me as I lay and, by the sound of my grunted response, came to be able to gauge the lapse of time before I got to my feet.

Whenever we were not on patrol, practice was carried out in bomb dropping. We used a marked out space at one end of the landing ground, shaped like a submarine, as a dummy target. At first we had little practice bombs and then 16-pounders which made a lovely bang but did not do much damage when dropped on our target submarine. One day, a sheep which had strayed on to the target area unnoticed, walked across the 'submarine' just as a bomb was released. Fortunately the sheep was not hit, but the explosion lifted it high off the ground. It appeared to continue moving its legs in mid-air and on landing just walked away!

We had no proper bombracks at first. I remember carrying a sheath knife to cut the string on which the bombs were slung; and our bombsights were at first a couple of wire nails. It was not long before we had 100-pounders charged with TNT, and later double that size, coupled with proper racks and fusing wires. And at last real bombsights — all of which the enemy submarines did their

Left: SS25, T.B. Williams' first command at Anglesey equipped with a BE2c car.

Below: the Car of SS10 at Wormwood Scrubs, being overhauled.

utmost to avoid. My original personal armament was a Webley-Scott pistol hanging on a brass cuphook, but this gave way to a Lewis machine gun in due course.

It was unwise to be too low, or to hang around too closely after releasing our bombs, as I found out by getting a splinter through my tail, or rather that of my ship, on one occasion.

In the Zeros we carried the larger bombs on each side of the pilot, under our arms as it were, and one could almost give them a friendly pat by way of a blessing when one fused and dropped them, and the ship leapt up in excitment when eased from their weight.

Our early SSs at Anglesey, although fitted with aeroplane fuselages as control cars, were more reliable than one would imagine. The Renault air-cooled engines gave little trouble as they were so carefully serviced by our reliable engineers. I was blessed with a series of the most faithful Coxwains imaginable, like Ashdown and Anness. I think of them with gratitude constantly and I owed much of my success and safe returns to their conscientious care of my ship – or I should say 'our' ship. The men who flew with me too, as gunner/wireless operators, I remember with affection; we shared the risks and hopes and fears. In those early days the wireless equipment was of the crudest and often broke down. Later, in the larger SSs of 70,000 cubic feet we were able to carry an engineer as well.

Numerous flights were carried out by the BE/SSs; I usually flew SS-25 but sometimes used one of the others if my ship was laid up and another was without a pilot.

My Log Book is crowded with records of flights along the trade routes into Liverpool; of escorting large convoys or scouting over areas in the Irish Sea where enemy submarines might be lurking. One can see deeper into water from the air than from the surface and the crew would be searching for a dark shadow below and for the tell-tale feather of water made by a periscope.

The Log records many minor troubles such as 'engine running very badly', 'very foggy at sea' and often 'dark night', 'very rough trip' or 'W/T broke down'; but somehow we managed to get home and get ready for the work of the next day or night.

On the 1st May 1917, I did my last flight with *SS-25* on a long trip south, to and fro over the Welsh coast ship routes, landing at Pembroke for refuelling. We left Anglesey at 6.20 in the morning, arriving back at 8.20 in the evening! I was asked recently: 'And when did you get a meal?' As the pilot could not leave his little bucket seat during a flight of often many hours duration, he just didn't get a meal. He was the Captain of the airship, but if it was an SS, in addition to passing messages to and from his wireless operator, he had to read his maps and compass and take bearings and work out his course. He had to watch his instrument panel with all its clocks and gauges, including pressure, time, height, inclination, direction, and so on. He had to steer with his feet, ascend or descend by a wheel in his right hand; attend to engine and ballonet controls with his left hand; watch the ocean on all sides at all times; and when the crucial moment arrived, squint through his bomb sight, fuse his bombs and drop them! There were a few hangers on, also, such as the trail rope, grapnel, sea drogue, water ballast tank, all controlled by the pilot, though there were no parachutes in those days.

Your dinner is served, sir!

Chapter 5

The S.S. Pusher Airships

Early in May 1917 I was ordered back to Wormwood Scrubs to take delivery of one of the new SSPs but found on arrival there that it was not yet ready, so I took the opportunity to complete the requirements for my *Federation Aeronautique Internationale* Airship Certificate, which was numbered 28. *SSP-6* was one of a series of six, the 'P' indicating a pusher; the car was a development of the Maurice Farman aeroplane fuselage formerly used with the engine in the rear; this car was therefore free from the slipstream of the propeller.

I was not happy at the thought of kicking my heels while waiting indefinitely so went up to the Airship Department of the Admiralty for a temporary job and was delighted when I was posted to Hurlingham as Assistant Balloon Instructor to Squadron Leader Pollock, flying in the *Polo, Swallow, May* and *Violet*.

On the 8th June, *SSP-6*, built at Wormwood Scrubs, was ready for trials which were successfully completed. A few days later I was instructed to fly down the River Thames to Kingsnorth, Chatham, as low over the water as was practical. I flew without an engineer, as the rear seat was to be occupied by a Senior Army officer on a mission, as to the nature of which I was given no information.

The day was hot, with many cumulus clouds and bumpy conditions. There was a great temptation to jump the bridges as I came to them, particularly Tower Bridge, but the weather conditions and the comfort of my guest restricted this.

I was very busy controlling the ship en route, and had no communication with the passenger behind me. I assumed that he was attending to the job of work alloted to him. At the mouth of the river I turned and looked behind me, but to my instant horror

SSP1 with the increased rudder plane surface; only six of these Pushers were built.

The crew of SSP6 round its Car. T.B. Williams is the central standing figure.

there was no sign of a passenger. When conditions permitted I half rose in my seat and peered over the back. My passenger was heaped on the floor, his complexion a nasty shade of green, and he was in a deplorable condition, whether from fear or air sickness I never knew. I could do nothing to help him, so I told my signaller to get in touch with Kingsnorth and ask if we could land. We soon had permission and our passenger was gently removed by the first aid department.

While waiting for instructions I went up to the officers' mess for refreshments and was subjected to some amused glances.

Then I went into the hangars to find out how the next SSP being built there was progressing, as I knew that there were to be six, and that it was likely that I should collect the next one from there. Soon after that, I had orders to return to Wormwood Scrubs and was told that my passenger would not be coming with me.

We had a delightful trip, returning over London with no one to hurry us, or harry us, and we gave the capital a treat as well as ourselves.

When I landed at the Scrubs I was told that the Commanding Officer wanted to see me in his office, to which I went immediately, searching my conscience for any misdeeds. To my relief I was received with amusement: Corbett-Wilson asked me if I had had a very rough and dangerous flight. I answered that it was a bit bumpy, but no worse than one would expect in the circumstances. He told me that he had received by telephone a dreadful tale of woe from Kingsnorth!

I liked my new airship quite well; she was a refinement on my original command, *SS-31* — 'The Flying Bedstead' — now missing from Kingsnorth.

The next day, 13th June 1917, we left Wormwood Scrubs for home early in the morning just as some German Gothas arrived over the Metropolis, but I flew low and northwards and was not molested. My sole armament was my faithful Webley-Scott pistol.

Two of my younger sisters were boarders at the Bluecoat School at Hertford, which was on my route north. I was able to let them know that I would be flying overhead and I found that all

Merchant ships being escorted through the Atlantic Approaches by airships.

the girls in the school appeared to be outside when I arrived. They were standing in a great circle on the playing field with the tiny figure of my youngest sister Celia in the centre, with the elder sister Irene near to her. I flew round above them several times and then slowed down and sat bow into the wind so that I could lean over and wave. The excitement was intense! – the girls jumping and cheering and waving like mad. I heard later that the status of my sisters had gone up immensely.

We landed at Cranwell in Lincolnshire, a new training station, at 10.40 with a broken keel-plane skid which had to be replaced; I was going to call there anyway to demonstrate the airship as a new type. The day and a half I spent at Cranwell was an eye-opener. It was the time when the Sopwith Camels were being put into service with young pilots in every stage of training. Camels were screaming all over the sky and appeared to be landing all over the aerodrome, sometimes upside down! I saw two fly into the ground and another hit the side of a hangar. I realized what the young pilots were going through: either one mastered the Camel or it mastered you. Even so, the Camel was one of the greatest aeroplanes of all time. John Pudney in *Camel Fighter** relates how Richthoven, the greatest of the German pilots, was shot down by a Canadian pilot, Captain A.R. Brown in a Camel. And the last Zeppelin to be shot down in the 1914-1918 war – *L-53* – was destroyed by Lieutenant S.D. Culley also in a Camel in August 1918 flying from a lighter towed by a destroyer. The *L-53* was at 19,000 feet when Culley, who could get no higher than about 300 feet below her, pulled back his stick and fired at the Zeppelin from underneath. One gun jammed, but the other sent a stream of bullets along the belly of the Zeppelin which caught fire. Culley had difficulty in finding his flotilla and had but a pint of petrol when picked up by his parent destroyer.

The Admiral sent a signal to his ships:

Camel Fighter by John Pudney, published by Hamish Hamilton, London 1964.

Hymns A & M No.224
> O happy band of pilgrims
> Look upward to the skies
> Where such a light affliction
> Shall win so great a prize.

But to return to my *SSP-6* at Cranwell. The ship was not ready until the afternoon of the next day when we left for Howden in Yorkshire. The water-pipe of the Green engine fractured in the air, but my engineer succeeded in effecting a temporary repair and we reached Howden early in the evening. We started for Barrow-in-Furness at crack of dawn the next morning but our water pipe fractured again and we had to return to Howden for repair, leaving once more in the evening and crossing England from east to west to land at the Vickers airship building station at Barrow-in-Furness late at night. We had a rough trip in the Leeds area with the unusual conditions of very bumpy weather and a thick fog. Leaving Barrow at 8 a.m the next day we were home at our base in Anglesey by 10.15. I always tried to start a journey as early as I could in the morning, particularly if I was on testing or experimental work, so that I had as much daylight as possible to get out of trouble if it occurred.

Obviously there is a shorter way between London and Anglesey than by the route I took, but there was a two-fold reason for my flying as I did. One was to show a new type of Submarine Searcher Airship to as many stations as was practical. Also with an untried airship it was prudent to make the flying legs as short as was possible. On this particular flight there were three breakages in the air, any of which could have been more serious if airship stations had not been so available; it must be remembered that I am writing of events which happened over fifty years ago.

Six SSPs were planned, but only three really reached the operational stage. Two were lost on delivery flights and, I believe, one in action. Eventually *SSP-1* and *SSP-5* were taken over by Anglesey as we seemed to be able to cope with my No.6. The engines were a constant headache, necessitating considerable work

T.B. Williams in the pilot's seat of SSP1.

T.B. Williams flying SSP6. The pilot is grasping the elevator wheel with his right hand. To the left of the elevator wheel are the aneroid dial and height indicator, and the third dial on the left is the clock. The compass is centrally placed at the top of the picture, and the dial to the left of the compass is a stop-watch. The pilot operated the rudder controls with his feet, and the engine controls are by the pilot's left hand. Overhead are other controls.

in maintenance and repair, but somehow I seemed to get along very well with *SSP-6* and carried out a good deal of the night flying.

It was a period of great fogs, for my log book is loaded with entries such as 'Thick fog all around coast', 'Island completely covered', 'Landed at dusk in very thick fog' and 'Thick fog, difficulty in finding Station, large flares burning on landing ground' — and so on. Our complement now was the three SSPs and my previous command, *SS-25* with a BE fuselage.

It is curious how often my log book tells of unusual happenings when flying one of the other two SSPs. In *SSP-5* for instance, on 3rd July: 'lost aerial in the sea . . . bombing wreckage to clear channel . . . landed with engine trouble'. There were two occasions when in my own ship *SSP-6* I stood by No.5 which had to force-land with engine trouble, on one occasion sustaining considerable damage.

Once when I was landing *SSP-1* the rudder jammed over the aerodrome; I was forced to balloon and came down on my rope, dropping my grapnel which closed when striking the ground, but dragged through a hedge, the jerk clearing the rudder. We started up the engine to return to base, but the magneto failed. We were able, however, to run on an accumulator and reach base in good style.

Another time my engine was running very roughly and threatened to stop, so I made a landing on a sports ground near Llandudno after dropping a note to the people playing games asking them to form a landing party. Coming down very gently with a stopped engine, I directed them through a megaphone. The experiment was very successful as the discipline of the helpers was admirable. In 35 minutes my engineer had found the trouble, put it right and we were away, amidst cheers.

By this time the RNAS had become short of airship pilots and it became normal for me to carry out instructional flights to 'pass out' pilots sent to us not yet fully trained. I often carried a 'quirk' in the rear cockpit instead of an engineer, particularly later in the Zeros.

At the beginning of November we were escorting American troop ships in, usually in very bad weather and often landing in the dark, after butting head-winds sometimes for hours. We were still having trouble with our engines, my log book having entries such as 'Landed owing to air lock in engine oil system' and 'Trouble with petrol system' and so on, interspersed with the usual records of bombing suspicious areas and so on.

The load was very heavy at this time. We were short of pilots and airships and there were many convoys crossing the Atlantic, but to our amazement in response to an appeal we received a message from the Admiralty that they were despatching six DH 4 aeroplanes to assist us. Our landing ground was quite unsuitable for aeroplanes and the only one of the flight to reach us struck a stone wall and the pilot was killed. We tried to salve another on the North Wales coast but the sea defeated our efforts.

In December a Senior Officer took *SSP-5* out at dawn on a trial flight. In his absence I was in charge of the station, as Senior Flying Officer.

After some hours I lost wireless touch with him and by the evening was contemplating reporting to the Admiralty that we had lost a boss, when a telegram arrived from Barrow-in-Furness, saying that the ship had landed there and instructing me to come and collect my 'bloody airship'. So I set off by night train to Barrow to be greeted by the W/T-Gunner and Engineer with some relief; the Chief had said that he would walk home. I flew the ship back to Anglesey the next morning in a thunderstorm which broke out on the way.

The day after my next birthday, the 16th January, I carried out trials after re-rigging my old *SS-25*. I had brought the fuselage as close to the envelope as was practicable and streamlined everything possible. The old lady had a new lease of life, but her days were numbered; we had heard whispers that the new SS Zeros were now on the stocks at Wormwood Scrubs and Kingsnorth, and then I was ordered to Kingsnorth again. While I was away a forced landing was made by *SSP-6* through engine failure near Blackburn in Lancashire and the airship was badly damaged.

SSP-1 and *SSP-6* were taken over by Cranwell as training ships, and soon all the patrolling from Anglesey and the escorting of the huge convoys coming from the Atlantic was carried out by SS Zeros.

As recently as 1966 Sam Charles sent me a broken propeller blade of *SSP-6*, of which he had been wireless operator, as he thought that I would be sure to give it a good home.

My job also included Courts of Enquiry, which could have meant a journey to Plymouth in connection with an event at Anglesey. One of our Petty Officers was charged with overstaying his leave. He stated that he had telephoned in the late evening and obtained permission from the duty officer of the time, but the latter seemed a bit vague about this call.

The matter was serious for the Petty Officer and the Commanding Officer who held a local enquiry postponed judgment until the next day. He suggested that the man should make a request for a 'prisoner's friend' to which he was entitled. the P/O asked for me.

I studied all the facts but could not see daylight. However, I knew the man well and felt that he was speaking the truth. I went to bed thinking that there must be evidence somewhere and awoke with the possible answer. I went to the telephone room and asked for the record of messages. In a few minutes I had found the entry. The Petty Officer was cleared and the journey to Plymouth avoided.

Chapter 6

The S.S. Zeros

Late in January 1918 I was posted to Kingsnorth once more, this time to fly a Zero, the latest type of SS, with which I spent many happy days.

The SSZs were dreams come true. I fell for them at once. They had narrow boat-shaped control cars especially built for airships with the engine at the rear and raised above the stern. Of 70,000 cubic feet capacity over the early SSs' 60,000, they gave us three cockpits of reasonable size and enabled us to carry bigger bombs, with bomb racks within reach. There was excellent visibility and a wide range of fire from the improved Lewis gun. I had always advocated having a boat-shaped body and here it was – and for good measure fitted with a Rolls-Royce Hawk engine.

In March I flew on the test flight of *SSZ-50*. I carried out the acceptance test the next day and later flew all over London for some hours dropping Victory Loan and War Bond leaflets. I used a dropping method that I had evolved when ballooning. Considerable care has to be exercised to keep clear of the airscrew as even a wad of paper could do considerable damage. Over the middle of a large city was no place to take any risk of this sort. I had done a number of flights over London both by airship and balloon and could pick out the streets without difficulty, so I was told to drop them at specific places; for instance, in front of the Mansion House, and in Trafalgar Square. I was frowned at when receiving instructions, for innocently asking if I should put them through the letter boxes!

In a few days I left Kingsnorth flying up the East Coast to Cranwell Training Station. I had wireless trouble on the way and landed at the aerodrome at Pulham Experimental Station in

Norfolk for repairs as I was out of communication with any station. The rectification took some hours to effect, but I decided to push on in the late afternoon as I was expected at Cranwell that day. I had to make a night landing at Cranwell, but this gave me no trouble. I had flown the ship for ten hours during the few days I had had her, and felt very much at home with my new steed.

Three days later, after *SSZ-50* had been closely inspected by the trainees, I once more took to the air, landing at Howden on the Yorkshire coast in the afternoon in a very thick mist.

During the night we were attacked by German Zeppelins. The noise was appalling as the air station at Howden was surrounded with anti-aircraft guns, and some of the Zeppelins' bombs were very close, a nearby village being badly punished.

Leaving Howden I crossed England from the North Sea to the Irish Sea passing over Barrow-in-Furness without landing and turned south for my base in Anglesey where I arrived in the early afternoon.

I flew the dawn patrol next morning in my new craft carrying out an eleven-hour flight over Liverpool Bay. I switched off my engine for a time and free-ballooned. I was getting to know and trust and love my beautiful airship and would shout and slap the flanks of the control car when we were charging into battle, much to the amusement of my crew. Two days later I flew another patrol over Liverpool Bay of more than eight hours and twice switched off and re-started the Rolls-Royce engine without difficulty. At last we had a trouble-free engine, and our engineers were able to get some sleep at nights.

On my next flight I carried out further tests with *SSZ-50*, alighting on the water and anchoring with a sea-drogue. I believe that this was the first time that an SS had alighted on the sea.

After escorting the Dublin Mail Steamer and other vessels across the Irish Sea, I taxied into Holyhead Harbour with the Mail but took her wash, got my crew very wet and caused enormous excitement on the steamer and amongst people gathered in the harbour.

That night we received a message from the Senior Naval Officer

c

The SS zero car which replaced the Maurice Farman and BE2c cars. The illustration shows how it constuction was adapted for the car to float like a boat. The lower picture shows the framework of the car.

at Holyhead saying that a steamer was being attacked by a submarine off the headland and asking if we could go to her assistance.

It was a very dark night with rain squalls and we were all very tired. I asked for a volunteer and then changed my mind and sent myself on the task. I could not find the darkened ship and when well down-wind received a message saying that she had crawled into the harbour at Holyhead.

I turned north-east into the gale making for Holyhead light, which by good fortune, or intentionally, was burning. I had no sense of movement in the pitch darkness and the screaming of the gale. A dread came over me that the wind was greater than my speed and that we were being driven out to sea — which fear I kept to myself. We seemed to be hours running through the black night before the light came nearer. Eventually I was right over it and turned on my course to the landing ground, the path of which was lighted by oil flares. The engine was running badly when I landed and I was very glad to get down. I found later that two exhaust valves were partially burnt out, but my Rolls-Royce engine had stuck it and brought me home.

Incidentally, I was finding the long patrols trying, inasmuch as it was difficult to answer the call of nature, the pilot not being able to leave his seat. I evolved an arrangement made up from a petrol funnel to which was attached a piece of rubber hose passing to a water tight junction in the hull under the seat. The petrol funnel was hung on a brass cup hook near my elbow and solved my problem. I had some difficulty in inventing a purpose for this gadget when explaining the instruments and controls to the wife of a VIP on one occasion!

Early in April, I collected the *SSZ-35* and on my first patrol on the 8th carried out a 7½-hour flight in the Liverpool Bay area and photographed the trenches on the Great Orme. I knew that we were short of fresh food at the aerodrome so on the way home sat down on the sea near a fishing boat and got the fishermen to bring us some fish in a row boat; the fresh fish hanging on a bomb-rack were received with acclaim when I landed. The rest of the month was spent in escorting some very large convoys into Liverpool, often combining the job with instructional flights for new pilots.

Before dawn on the 26th April I had left my base in Anglesey and during the morning was searching off Liverpool for a German submarine reported in the area. Soon after 10 o'clock I was near the Formby Lightship and had just received a message that the submarine had been sighted nearby when my engine stopped. I ballooned for a short time, but we found that the engine had seized up and could not be restarted. I then came down onto my trail rope with the drogue attached to slow up my drift towards the mountains of North Wales as the wind was from the north-west.

I had previously sent a message to base which had also been picked up by a nearby Pilot Boat which replied that it was coming to our assistance. The Pilot Boat arrived in company with an armed trawler. I requested a tow to Holyhead and my rope was taken over by the trawler which set off towards Anglesey by noon, of which my base was duly informed.

The airship was out of shape through some loss of gas when coming down onto the drogue so did not tow very well. During the tow the engine was found to be easier, but repeated attempts to start it were unsuccessful. The wind increased later and the airship was difficult to handle. We passed through banks of fog on the way which made us heavy and water ballast was dropped to compensate. The ship swung about sharply and several times the trawler had to ease or stop to prevent us striking the water.

Eventually I decided to jettison a 100-pound bomb to keep us light, which was effective for a time. The aerial could be used occasionally and I asked base if I should try for Redwharf Bay, on the north coast of Anglesey.

At about three o'clock I sighted the Great Orme and sent a message through *SSZ-34* which had appeared on the scene suggesting that I tried to get into Llandudno. I had a message of agreement and the welcome news that a party of soldiers in Llandudno would render assistance; in due course they took over the trail rope from the trawler at the end of the pier, walked the

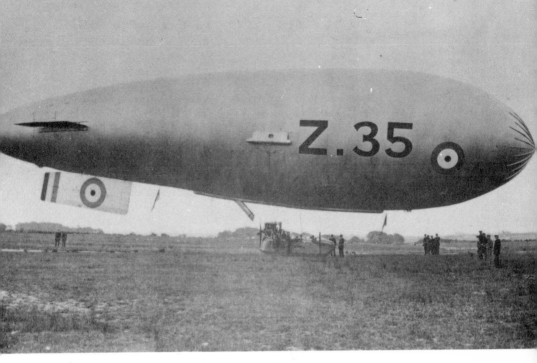

T.B. Williams' favourite SSZ 35 landing at Anglesey.

The Royal Naval Airship Station at Anglesey, which was operational from 1915-1918.

ship to the beach and soon after five I was moored between two hotels on the promenade.

When pulling me down to earth, one of the soldiers bent down and picked up a fusing wire that had fallen from a bomb rack, the one from which I had dropped the bomb out at sea when I was being towed. I realized with a shock that had I not had the foresight to send the Engineer over the side to safety-pin the bombs when the engine failed, both the trawler and ourselves would have been destroyed. The tow rope had twisted the bomb rack and I had dropped that bomb live!

Soon after we had tied down on Llandudno promenade, the breakdown party from Anglesey arrived, including the welcome faces of the Engineer Officer and my own Coxswain. They had a lorry-load of everything required and appeared at a considerable speed with hooters sounding loudly. The crowd of people milling around seemed enormous and the police had some difficulty in keeping them back. Eventually the airship area was roped round and everyone was warned of the fire danger, with such a quantity of petrol and hydrogen in evidence.

There were many visitors in Llandudno and I was bothered somewhat by a procession of visiting cards and requests for a nearer view.

Soon gas was hissing into the envelope of the ship, which quickly took up its usual alert appearance when the creases disappeared. Reaching the high petrol tanks on the flanks of the airship created a problem, but inspiration came and I asked for the services of the local fire brigade with its turn-table ladder, which was immediately forthcoming.

A kind invitation came from the Hydro Hotel to which in a sense I was attached, to take dinner there and a bath. I was in a disgusting state, the airship was secure and in good hands, so I gratefully accepted. When dressing after my wash I found that I had no tie, but was lent one by the hotel manager. It was very gaudy for a Naval Officer and caused considerable amusement.

When I got back to my trusty steed, the engine had been overhauled including taking down the water pump, which I was told had caused the trouble. About eight o'clock in the evening, the engine was restarted. I flew off the beach half an hour later, reaching my base in Anglesey in about forty minutes.

I came in to land just at the quiet of dusk and just before landing lights were really necessary. I was able to relax at last securely in the hands of the landing party, although the engine had stopped again on my run in.

Then came a voice from the ground that was the last straw to my control. I cannot think of it to this day without emotion, though I never knew whose voice it was, 'Three cheers', it said 'for Bloody Bill'. The roar that followed shook me to the core. It was the first time that I had heard my lower deck name, but it was spoken, and responded to, with affection.

The very next day after the engine had been overhauled I took the ship up in the evening with the Station Engineer Officer in the 'back seat'. The engine seized up again ten minutes after leaving the ground and the ship drifted over the station at 800 feet. I had observed my usual practice of flying to windward whenever possible on trials or experimental work. Gas was valved and the grapnel dropped when a suitable position was reached, only about three miles from the station. The grapnel caught in a hedge and the ship swung violently sideways and downwards. When a few feet above the ground, the passenger was instructed to jump out and try and keep the grapnel from coming adrift. This was accomplished with the aid of a woman from a nearby cottage. On the arrival of a number of civilians the ship was hauled down and farm labourers instructed how to keep her bow into wind by means of the handling guys. Soon afterwards a party arrived from the station. It was found possible a little later to run the engine sufficiently to blow the ship up to pressure. The ship was then let up on the trail rope and walked across country back to the shed without damage.

I must have had a spot of leave just then as I find that the next entry in my log book is dated 7th May with a ten-hour patrol over Liverpool Bay. Our doctor watched the pilots carefully, so perhaps, I had been showing some signs of strain. I seem to

Left: SSZ 35 moored at Llandudno after engine failure.

Below: the car of an SS zero showing 1 cwt bombs in position at the side of the car, the camera behind the cockpit and a Lewis machine gun mounted forward.

remember going to Liverpool about this time to see what it looked like from inside instead of from outside. Or perhaps I went and had another dinner at the Hydro in Llandudno where I had had such an excellent meal when I was towed in with *SSZ-35*.

I think that it must have been about this time also that after sitting in heavy rain for some hours on end, on landing I had to be lifted out of my seat in a sitting position. It was days before I could be straightened out and I suffered from occasional bouts of sciatica for years. This finally disappeared when I fell and struck my thigh on a rock beside the Exploits River in Newfoundland several years afterwards.

I think that I must dare to blow my own trumpet here. I was able to pass-out all but one of the partly trained pilots sent to us by Cranwell; this one was a problem but I got permission to use him to work out an idea I had developed, and that was a hush-hush information hut, where all the information received about the position of convoys, warship movements and enemy activities were kept on wall charts, and up-to-date to the last minute. The incidents on the 18th and 19th May 1918 were the direct results of keeping dates of enemy activities, or so I believe. I noticed that reports from off Bardsey Island, where the steamer track changed direction, appeared to occur at more or less fixed periods. Could it be a submarine going home for fuel? Remember it was 1918. I considered that it was likely that there would be some action again probably at dawn and about the 18th of the month. It may be that I was guessing, if so it was a lucky one.

There was considerable enemy activity during the summer of 1918 and we were also closely watching the area round the Skerries, as well as Bardsey Island, where the steamer track took another turn through the Irish Sea.

Early in the morning of the 18th May we had three airships over these areas; one of them patrolling the Skerries lane observed a stream of oil forming on the water and moving in a westerly direction. A 100-pound bomb was dropped and later a 230-pounder from a greater height resulting in a violent underwater explosion. The other two airships were very quickly on the scene and joined in the attack, with a British destroyer. The destroyer was, I think, *DO-1* which worked with us and with which I was often in communication. I never actually met her Commanding Officer but at times we had long conversations by Aldis lamp. *SSZ-51* returned to base, but Campbell and I stayed to photograph the area. I alighted on the surface of the sea and took oil samples for analysis. The destroyer considered that we had made a kill.

I decided to search the Bardsey Island area next day, as my dates seemed to indicate possible activity there. Three airships were strung out along the trade route before dawn and at 0430 as the sun rose *SSZ-51* observed oil bubbles rising to the surface and then a periscope and the dark hull of a submarine travelling in a south-westerly direction. A message was sent out to this effect, giving the position 52.42 N. 5.03 W.

SSZ-51 made sufficient height and planted a 230-pound bomb closely. I was very quickly on the scene and followed suit.

An American destroyer, No.20, arrived on the scene and dropped depth charges in the area we indicated, followed by two more American destroyers, Nos. 40 and 66, which dropped further depth charges. Vast quantities of oil bubbles appeared covering the surface for over a mile, followed by debris. I stayed with the destroyers searching, while the other two airships returned to base. The British destroyer *DO-1* joined the Americans and between them they knocked the bottom out of the sea. I was almost shaken to pieces by the tremendous explosions.

We were given this later as a confirmed kill; usually the destroyers got the credit for submarines destroyed, although perhaps we had found them and struck the first blow.

On the 20th and 21st May I did long patrols with the destroyers over the steamer lanes turning at Bardsey Island. There were no further reports of attacks at that time on the shipping there. In the same area later in the month, I spotted considerable wreckage and attempted to get onto the water to pick up a large lifebuoy. I was unsuccessful in this because of the rough sea. I shipped part of a green wave into the control car and was thankful to get off.

A light cruiser, HMS *Patrol* had now taken over the lead of our surface craft and I often acted as the air scout in 'SSZ-35'. The *Patrol* was in charge of Commander Gordon Campbell, RN, who it was said was the most decorated man in the Navy, with a VC downwards. He became famous for his work with Q-boats, that is, harmless and helpless looking merchant vessels which were really naval vessels armed to the teeth — as many enemies found to their cost.

I was very impressed by an incident on the 25th May when I flew off from base soon after 4 o'clock in the morning to meet the HMS *Patrol* and two destroyers bringing a convoy out of Liverpool bound for Kingstown. Half way across the Irish Sea while I was flying to and fro ahead of the convoy I spotted something in the water. I came down low and flew in small circles but could not determine what it was; it should not be there I was sure. I therefore sent a message to the *Patrol* saying: 'Suspicious object beneath me, in your track'.

Almost immediately, as though I had pressed a button, all the surface craft changed course and scattered. I was climbing higher to get a better overall picture and range for my signals, when a noise like an express train rushed underneath me, and my ship bounced in the air. The *Patrol* had opened fire; which disturbed my 'suspicious object' not at all. Soon the gunfire ceased and while one destroyer was running round the convoy like a dog rounding up sheep, the other raced towards the circled offender, and warily circled it. This destroyer then stopped and lowered a boat which in turn went round and round in ever smaller circles. Eventually the boat went alongside and dragged the culprit on board with many attachments. The boat returned to the destroyer and the convoy was brought back onto its course with the destroyers out on the wings and my airship out ahead followed by HMS *Patrol*.

Then a message came from the *Patrol*: 'Your suspicious object is a fisherman's buoy'.

Some time afterwards I was talking to Commander Campbell and I said to him, with reference to this trip: 'I'm afraid that I caused a flurry when I scattered your fleet, sir'. He looked at me quietly for a few moments as though sizing me up and I wondered what was coming. Then he replied: 'On the contrary. We were very grateful for the sharp eyes ahead. It might have been something very different'.

We got the convoy safely into Kingstown and I flew on to the mooring-out station that we had formed at Malahide, north of Dublin, among the trees of Malahide Castle, the residence of Lord Talbot. I stayed in a tent on the edge of the landing ground. I was to have left with a convoy to Liverpool the next day but a great blanket of fog came down and it was decided to delay departure for a day longer after I had made a short flight to reconnoitre.

The next day there was a thick mist on the sea but high overhead a blue sky and bright sun. Everything started to move with the ships on the surface of the water hidden from me. I found that their black smoke rose to the top of the bank of mist lying on the water and was able to follow the track of the steamers without difficulty. Half way across the Irish Sea the mist suddenly cleared and the fact that I was flying to and fro over them at that time was considered skilful navigation.

I let Captain Birch, the Commander of the Irish Mail steamer which was amongst those escorted, into the secret when I next saw him. He and I had become friends as we were on and over the Irish Sea so often together. I took him for a flight in *SSZ-35* on the 1st June, and he arranged with the Triplex Company, of which he was a shareholder, to send me some flying goggles which I still have. When I was flying with the Italians later in the year I was sent an account of his death, which I found very distressing. He had been blown off the bridge of the Irish Mail Steamer by a German torpedo.

On the last day of the month I had engine trouble while flying over Liverpool Bay again and landed on the sports ground at Llandudno, found the trouble and carried on patrol. I was glad to have the break, as one got very tired on these long patrols.

Off Southport once I was close inshore and saw there a fair-ground. One of the amusements was a roundabout with boat-cars like miniature airships. As the roundabout revolved the cars swung out wider and wider until they were almost on their

The armed Trawler BCK 912 towing SSZ 35 in Liverpool Bay towards Llandudno.

Picking up a lifebuoy from the Irish Sea in SSZ 35 in 1918.

Far right: the actual lifebuoy on display at Anglesey Airship Station.

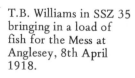

T.B. Williams in SSZ 35 bringing in a load of fish for the Mess at Anglesey, 8th April 1918.

sides, the occupants being kept stuck to their seats presumably by centrifugal force. This was too much for me, so I joined the procession flying round and round outside the little cars, and a good time was had by all!

One evening while flying from Malahide, I alighted on the water at 52.22 N, 5.10 W and picked up a large lifebuoy without a name, carrying it to Anglesey hanging on the Lewis gun rack. Whether it was connected with our numerous bombings or not I could not tell. It was later beautifully painted and mounted on the quarter deck outside the officers mess at Anglesey.

Patrolling and attacking was continued during the month. On the 4th I dropped a 230 lb. bomb fused, but it failed to explode. It was about this time that I lost my old naval service cap overboard. It had become soft and comfortable and I wore it in preference to my flying helmet which I suppose I shouldn't have done. I viewed the fall with great dismay as I had promised the little bird on it to my mother for a brooch. I shouted to my gunner that I was going down after it as I could see it floating. He raked out a weapon from his cockpit in no time and as I gently taxied up to the cap on the water, he flicked it into the control car.

Malahide Mooring-out Station became extremely useful to us, and I often landed there and used it as my base. We were received with very mixed feelings by the local inhabitants. One man who lived very close to the gates of our castle sent me a message saying that there was a bedroom and bath always available in his house; I could just go in and help myself. There were others who didn't like us at all. We had no telephone at Malahide at first and had to go to the local police station for messages. When returning on one occasion in the sidecar of a motor cycle, our only ground transport at the time, our speed was increased by a hail of bullets, which fortunately did us no damage. I was told that they did not like my naval uniform. Some time after that our ancient Ford, running with supplies from Dublin, was waylaid with a rope across the road. Both the driver and the van were damaged, but not irreparably.

There was a more subtle method of coercion. A row of men would sit silently on the boundary wall and just stare. It sounds nothing, but when this goes on hour after hour, day after day, it became too much for some who had to endure it. I was usually away in the air but a Petty Officer who looked after ground affairs could stand it no longer and I had to fly him back to base.

I remember being in a police station in Ireland waiting for a telephone call; looking idly out of the window I saw a group of men playing pitch and toss, with some money passing. I said to the Sergeant: 'Isn't it illegal to gamble in the streets?'

'Yes, sir' answered the Sergeant. 'But while they are doing that they are not doing anything worse'.

On 16th June I carried out the flight trials on *SSZ-51*, which we had re-rigged, and did several flights in *SSZ-34* as my own craft was receiving a much needed overhaul. I was back in *SSZ-35* by the 19th and working with HMS *Patrol*. On the 23rd my wireless broke down and I had to receive and transmit through the cruiser.

We had some superb weather at the end of June, which was an opportunity I had been waiting for to try and make a record flight. With Lieutenant Farina in the engineer's seat and Air Mechanic Rawlins as W/T Operator/Gunner, I took off at 0445 in *SSZ-35* on the 29th flying as slowly as I could across the Irish Sea, turning north up the Irish Coast to Scotland, back to the Isle of Man and east to the English coast, flying over Blackpool and Southsea for a break and turning south towards Liverpool. Then along the north coast of Wales turning south again at Holyhead over Caernarvon Bay and down the west coast of Wales. Farina and I took spells in the pilot's seat, but we found that changing seats was rather a difficult task. We had to climb out of our own seat and into the other fellow's cockpit; by putting the rudder hard over and the elevators amidship, we managed the scramble.

Strangely perhaps, I found that when I was piloting I wanted to take tiny cat naps as I got more tired, but when I changed over into the rear seat, I became wide awake at once, staring about me and watching the instruments over Farina's shoulder.

The long day passed and the night with another brilliant day and a welcome warm sun. We were tired and bored.

We had turned north again and were off the west coast of Anglesey when Farina asked if he could try and drop one of the smaller bombs of those we carried on an offshore rock. I agreed, but we were tired and careless. Travelling too slowly and too low, a splinter went through our envelope just missing me and we had to hurry home, which fortunately was not far away, getting down onto the aerodrome before we were forced down. We had, however, broken the record for a single-engined airship with a flight of twenty-six hours and ten minutes. Imagine my chagrin when I found that I had used only a little over half of my petrol, the gauge being faulty.

After a number of times alighting on the sea in the course of my patrolling work, related previously, in which I recovered my naval cap lost overboard, picked up a lifebuoy, a deck chair, oil samples, rode to a drogue, brought in a load of fish and taxied into Holyhead with the Irish Mail steamer, the Authorities were at least convinced that the SS Zero would really float on the water.

On the 5th July I carried out my last flight at Anglesey, in my beloved *SSZ-35*. There was great news: the British Government had bought a semi-rigid airship from the Italians and I, as Chief Officer to Captain G.F. Meager, was appointed to the crew going to collect her from Rome.

Chapter 7

Anglesey Reminiscences

The arduous hours of hunting submarines from our Anglesey base were broken periodically by happenings of a lighter nature; indeed, the station doctor who visited us from time to time encouraged us, or rather ordered us, to get a change of conditions whenever possible. Mess fighting was a popular sport, of course, releasing some of the local petty grievances. One dreadful Sunday — strange that I should remember that it was a Sunday — when a screaming gale with torrents of rain shook the mess to its foundations and flying was impossible, the pilots sat about reading and talking after getting tired of 'ginning the seagulls'. This consisted of soaking scraps of bread in the remains of glasses of beer, wine or spirits and throwing them to the seagulls which were sheltering from the wind to leeward of the mess. Like human beings after drinking too much they became either quarrelsome, loving or depressed. One old veteran with bedraggled feathers held forth like a Hyde Park orator. None of the others listened to him very much. They were too concerned for themselves, either in being sick, squawking for more food, or just being morose or affectionate.

One or two brave birds, fired with Dutch courage, took off into the gale, but soon lost control and hastily attempted to land. One landed with starboard wing low and a puzzled expression. Another tried to land upside down with uncomfortable results. At least one other almost damaged his undercarriage. I laughed till I cried. They gave up gobbling up our gifts after a time and huddled in a corner attempting to sleep it off.

Then came the sound of the gramophone playing — I think the name of the title is right: Lee White singing *That Wonderful*

Island. We had an officer who had transferred from seaborne ships to airships and tried to be superior about it, which attitude others did not like. We had heard this tune of his dozens of times. This time it was one too many. A great roar went up as a rush was made towards the gramophone with the owner stoutly defending it. At once attacking and defending parties were formed which swayed to and fro round the unfortunate gramophone. Eventually the record was dropped out of the window and an attempt made to drop the owner on top of it. Some of his supporters went outside and tried to push him back through the window. The fight went on with him being pushed in and out of the window in torrents of rain and occasionally falling into the mud of what had been a flower bed. The record had now been completely destroyed and the attackers, being now satisfied, returned to their chairs and ordered another drink. Sleep descended upon us, interrupted by a conversation between two members as to their relationship; they had discovered that they had both had the same girl for a sweetheart.

A favourite form of sport was called 'debagging', that is the removal of an offender's trousers and preventing him from obtaining a replacement until honour was satisfied. One pilot named Carver, whenever a riot started, would climb up into the rafters out of harm's way and sit there indefinitely like a broody hen; I would enter the mess after a long patrol and seeing Carver perched up under the roof would know that there was something brewing. Usually being tired out and having had as much fighting as I could do with for that day, I would retire to a bath, food and bed.

The long suffering piano, which was often included in a round of drinks and given its glass of beer, would shake to some rousing and bawdy chorus, the whole scene rocking with male vigour and the trembling tenseness of danger.

One of our bright sporting days at Anglesey was when Bangor Girls' College challenged the officers mess to play hockey against them. They would provide the sticks, which they did. On the way to Bangor there were several remarks about the need to be gentle with the girls and so on. As soon as the game started, however, we realized that the boot was on the other foot. Howls of agony arose from our damaged players as the ball tore through the ranks at express speed. We lost count of the goals scored against us and were glad to give them best. They however, gave us a grand tea and we retired to a pub in the town carrying our wounded with us. I thought that I should never walk without a limp again, my legs were so hacked. A missing piece of shin bone left with a balloon some years before did not improve matters.

I believe that it was on this occasion that after painting the town a very pale shade of pink some of us hired a taxi. Petrol was scarce and drivers scarcer. Our driver appeared to be over a hundred years old. His taxi was a T Model Ford — one of those early ones which went astern if you pressed a certain pedal; I don't remember which now. What a journey! We started by nearly missing the opening to Menai Bridge and narrowly escaped dropping into Menai Straits. We were challenged by a sympathetic policeman. I did the heavy with a Welsh name and an attempt at a Welsh accent. Having got past him and the exit to the bridge the old gentleman driving us tried to climb hedges and walls with the Tin Lizzie. On being questioned he admitted that he couldn't really see and had a go at any hole he saw. I took over at this, with only slightly better success. No one seemed to care very much and we eventually arrived back at base, rather the worse for wear.

Our nearest town in Anglesey was Llangefni, where we had many friends. A family named Trevor-Williams (may their name be blessed) kept open house for us. Many the happy party we had there. Two of the pilots who were at the Station when I arrived, Kilburn and Dixon, and who were inseparable, could often be found there being entertained by the charming daughters of the house and their girlfriends. My flying partner of that time, Elliott, who was afterwards killed in *NS-11* when working on mine-sweeping with the Navy, married one of the girls named Hazel. I had the sad task of breaking the news to her. Some time afterwards Dixon was shot down in the North Sea by a German seaplane, believed to be a Hansa-Brandenburg flown by Christiansen, pilot in charge at Zeebrugge, while flying airship C-27. Kilburn his mate, in C-26 searched for him until he ran out of petrol, when he force-landed in Holland and the crew were interned.

We found it difficult to repay our kind hosts in Llangefni, but one evening when we went ashore in the liberty boat, that is, to Llangefni in the Crossley tender, a hare ran into one of our wheels and we were able to present this to Mrs Trevor on our arrival. This was a change from the box of chocolates — if and when we could get one.

Sometimes in the evenings concerts would be organized in one of the mess huts and whatever talent we had was produced to cheer or amuse our fellows. I remember acting as a comedian on several occasions, chanting songs such as Goosey, Goosey, Gander, with a goose manufactured in the fabric shop stuffed with sawdust provided by the carpenters. Occasionally we were very lucky indeed, as once when we found that a newcomer had been an opera singer at Covent Garden. I was outshone very soon by a real comedian's arrival.

There was talk again of carrying parachutes, but without it being expressed in so many words I think that it would have been considered as rather 'cissie', although we did use one once. When coming in to land on the aerodrome I often passed over my cottage, to which I retired when circumstances permitted. On one occasion I had been presented with a nice fat rabbit in Malahide. My crew rigged up a little parachute on the way across the Irish Sea and we dropped the body on to the lawn in front of the door, to the wonder of upturned faces.

While I was in Italy later I heard from Anglesey that a young flying officer, who had been told that TNT was quite safe to handle if not detonated, thought that he would like the casing of a small bomb as a souvenir. So he hung one upside down by the blacksmith's fire in a workshop near the airship hangar. It did not go according to plan. There was a very big bang. No one was hurt, fortunately, but the explosion did not do either the shed or the airships any good.

Left: Flight Commander Tommy Elmhirst, C.O. at Anglesey 1918. *Right:* T.B. Williams in normal flying kit going on patrol from Anglesey in 1917.

SS 25 being towed home by *Amethyst.*

I saw four Commanding Officers and five First Lieutenants at Anglesey during my eighteen months there. I must record a vote of thanks to our visiting Padre and Doctor at Anglesey, both of whom attended to us so conscientiously; and so skilfully avoided innumerable drinks passed to them at the wrong time.

On Sundays, for those of us who were available, the Padre would open up a little folding altar in one of the huts. I can remember it so clearly. In the centre was a beautifully painted little airship flying in the clouds. Above it the words *He did fly upon the wings of the wind* and below *Underneath are the everlasting arms.* (Psalm 18-10, Deut. 33-27).

I think that this may be a convenient place to relate the story of the adventure of a very early pilot flying *SS-18* in Anglesey related by Air Marshal Sir Victor Goddard, who was himself a junior officer at the time of the event. In 1972 Air Marshal Sir Victor Goddard was elected President of the Airship Association: while Lord Ventry and I were elected as two of the Vice Presidents.

The account was originally printed by *Shell Aviation News*, which publication has kindly given me permission to reprint this gem in my book.

'Mr. Wu' – William Urquart by name – was a sub lieutenant, Royal Navy, Captain of *SS-18*, officially an Airship Submarine Searcher, unofficially a Blimp. When many years ago, I asked Mr. Wu to confirm the truth of the story I am about to tell, he said that some of the facts were exaggerated, but he didn't say which. Mr. Wu is a very modest man and I suggest that it is Mr. Wu's modesty which is the exaggerating factor – not my imagination.

At the end of 1915, U-boat sinkings of merchant ships had become really alarming. Although, on the one hand, when there was an airship in the vicinity no ships had been sunk or even attacked by U-boats, on the other hand, not many submarines had been seen and attacked by us, the airship fraternity, so we had no grounds for satisfaction. We had been acting simply as 'animated scarecrows'. Submarine captains could see us through their periscopes; they mistakenly supposed that we could see them.

Mr. Wu, based at the new airship station in Anglesey, North

Wales, made his daily patrols over the Irish Sea and concealed his frustrated spirit under a mild manner. One day, he decided that day-time patrols weren't good enough; he would fly out by night to the northern focus of shipping routes for the Mersey and be there just before dawn. There, he would find U-boats on the surface recharging their batteries; he'd catch 'em unawares, before they could submerge for their day long stealthy tracking of the merchant ships. To fly a blimp at night was something new. Mr. Wu chose a good night for his first attempt to justify this daring change of tactics.

Just before setting out, Mr. Wu found that his wireless operator had gone sick. Leading Mechanic Sparks, a new arrival, was detailed to take his place. The fact that Sparks had never been up in an airship before didn't transpire at that moment. No time then for personal chit chat. Away they went, Mr. Wu and Sparks, in their little airship — well, when I say 'little' I mean only 120 feet long — away into the calm cold midnight darkness, and set course nor'-nor'-west. And nothing more was heard of them until nearly breakfast time. But I'd better tell you what Sub-Lieutenant Nicholson of the Armed Yacht *Cynthia* had to say.

The *Cynthia* was a motor yacht, commandeered by the Admiralty, and put on anti submarine patrol duties in the Irish Sea. Nicholson was in the dimly lighted wheelhouse taking a trick at the wheel in the middle watch. The only others on deck, out of the whole ship's company of twelve, were two seamen manning the three-pounder gun on the fo'c'sle. There was a fresh breeze from the south-west and spray was coming over. It was dark and very cold. Nicholson had shut himself into the wheelhouse. At about 2 a.m he was aware of a face at the port side window a ghastly, anxious face, not the face of any member of that little ship's company. The strange face, which was wet with spray and white as a sheet, was surrounded by a rim of black, like a flying helmet. It was peering into the dim wheelhouse. Now Nicholson was a young Sub-Lieutenant, not long at sea. Here was the realization of his worst fear, a sea ghost. The seen, but unseeing, stranger banged on the window with his fist. Nicholson, mastering

T.B. Williams landing SSZ 35 at Anglesey.

A group of Officers at Anglesey.

his fears, flung open the door and cried: 'Who the devil are you, and what d'you want?'

'Leading Mechanic Sparks, sir, wireless operator of *SS-18* just crashed on the after rail of your quarter deck, sir. She's caught by the undercarriage, sir. Please come and see!'

Nicholson peered aft into the night and there, looming above the stern and towering up dark against the swaying stars was the great envelope of a semi deflated airship, dwarfing the yacht that it had floundered upon.

Well there she was: *SS-18*.

'Anyone with you?' asked Nicholson.

'No, sir, I left the Captain on the top of a tree in a wood an hour ago. Can you send a wireless message for me, sir'.

'No. No wireless', said Nicholson. 'Quartermaster. Muster the watch on deck. We'll make your ship fast where she is and put back to Holyhead. What made you pick on us?' Sparks explained that he had no choice and he made none. He'd been wafted up into the sky, till he'd nearly frozen to death and then come swooning down and here he was. And I still have the photograph of the *Cynthia* back in Holyhead with the disabled *SS-18* clinging to her stern, like a half filled sausage, nose high in the air, tail bedraggled and draped over the deck.

Well, now, we must attend to Mr. Wu. Not long after setting out, the engine had overheated itself and conked out. No unusual happening this. *SS-18* thus became a free balloon and would soon be drifting helplessly over the Irish Sea unless she could be brought to ground at once. Grabbing the cord to the top gas valve Mr. Wu tugged it to release the hydrogen that kept the ship afloat, and set about making a balloon landing in what, on that moonless night, looked like a big dark field. To check his rate of fall, Mr. Wu released a good whack of water ballast. Alas, the chosen 'field' turned out to be a big, dark, wood. Softly, with a crackling of twigs and rustling of leaves, the ship nestled in the tree tops, buoyant and restless but momentarily secured by the branches' embrace. Nimble as a rigger, out got Mr. Wu on to the starboard undercarriage skid. First, he released the trailrope and made it fast to the skid and to a nearby branch. Then, with the aid of the rope he swung himself on to the bough below, grabbed hold and sat himself down. Immediately, thereby, the ship gained buoyancy — by losing the dead load of Mr. Wu — and up she lifted herself out above the treetops, tethered to the branch.

'That's got her!' cried Mr. Wu triumphantly. 'Now make a signal to base'.

'Fraid my aerial's carried away, sir' replied Sparks apologetically.

But Mr. Wu was preoccupied. Once clear above the trees the ship in the breeze began to tug at her moorings; the rope held but the gusts nagged. The ship was raring to go. Next moment with a crack and a snap, away she went with her trophy of beech and that unfledged aeronaut, Leading Mechanic Sparks.

'What do I do now, sir?' wailed Sparks, receding into the night. 'I've never been up before'.

'Climb over into my seat and pull the gas valve cord', yelled Mr. Wu. 'But don't pull the rip cord or you'll break your neck'.

'Aye aye, sir, but which is which? I can't see. . . .' His voice was drowned by the rustling of the wind in the trees . . . but we needn't spend any more sympathy on Sparks, for, as we know, he was luckier than he had any right to expect. What goes up, must come down. Mr. Wu was now in a hurry. Something must be done to rescue the unhappy Sparks who was certain to come down in the drink.

Mr. Wu began to climb down, branch by branch in the dark, feeling with his toes. Then there were no more branches. Should he jump?

No. He was a sailor — he'd take soundings first. He took off his long woollen scarf, and then took off one of his sea boots, tied the two together, held the end of the scarf and plumbed for bottom. No bottom!

Mr. Wu took off his leather flying coat belt, lengthened the lead line and plumbed again. No bottom! Mr. Wu reluctantly took off his flying coat, and tied it on by one arm. No bottom! Then his jacket and his sweater. Still, no bottom! 'Nothing else for it' thought Mr. Wu, 'I'll have to put my trousers on the line. That should make about 3 fathom'. But yet, still no bottom!

Finally, shivering with cold, Mr. Wu, clad in his underpants, two socks, one seaboot and a flying helmet, decided he'd have little hope of organizing Sparks' rescue if he jumped down twenty feet or so in the dark, so he tied his 'lead line', his life line, with his vest and shirt to the bough he was sitting on, and began to climb down his rope of garments.

Trousers, sweater, jacket, leather coat, belt, scarf, sea boot. Mr. Wu let himself down until he dangled by his hands from the ankle of that boot. No bottom!

Mr. Wu no longer greatly cared. He let go. He fell — only about 6 feet, so he hardly hurt himself. Then he realized — no clothes!

Chattering with cold Mr. Wu set off in the dark; one boot on, one boot up the tree. Bang; he ran into a tree. He set off again — bang into another tree. He reeled back and tried again. Bump! The wood was black as ink and full of trees. Dazed, bruised and bewildered Mr. Wu tripped and fell full length and was ready to die. He was lying on dry leaves. Beech leaves! He was a babe in the wood! Blindly, and in a frenzy, he scuffled up leaves till he'd made a great heap of them, an invisible but tangible heap — and then he got inside.

First light came at about 7 a.m. It was winter time, remember. When it was light enough to run, aching and anxious, Mr. Wu scrambled out of his bed and set off as fast as he could, dot and carry one. Soon he was out of the wood and into a lane. Mr. Wu is reticent about what occurred in that lane. Let's leave him there — hobbling along, flapping his arms. He was taken care of quite soon.

The search party from the Airship Station, alerted by the report from Holyhead eventually found Mr. Wu locked in a bedroom of a cottage belonging to an old widow — Mrs Trevor Jones — who seemed to have no word of English. Mr. Wu could speak no Welsh. And it was Mr. Thomas, the farmer, who called the Police.

It was war time and Mr. Thomas employed landgirls. As a quartette of them going to work came round the corner down the lane by the wood, they saw a man with one boot and little else, prancing along, flapping his arms. Seeing the girls, the strange creature turned tail and fled. The girls gave chase. Then, finding a timely gate in the hedge Mr. Wu lept over, and jumping close to the hedge, thrust his helmeted head over the top and announced with breathless gravity: 'I am an airship Captain. I have lost my airship!' So the girls knew that he was an escaped lunatic and that's why they captured him and soothed him while he chattered out his nightmare tale and then got Mrs Jones to lock him up, until Mr. Thomas could get the Police.

Chapter 8

The Royal Air Force is Born

On the 1st April 1918 the Royal Air Force was born, and personnel of the Royal Flying Corps and the Royal Naval Air Service were transferred to the new organization. Officers were re-commissioned. At first it made little difference to us. We still wore our old naval monkey jackets and comfortable peaked caps, usually much battered.

A difficulty arose when Army officers and Navy officers became mixed together and ranks became involved. In the airship service it was not so awkward as there were no army airship officers, but in the aeroplane services confusion arose at once. A naval officer ranked one step higher than an army officer and at first this step was marked by adding a star to one's rank if ex-navy. This was disliked by all concerned as being not self-explanatory. Eventually the naval Flight Lieutenants were ranked as Captains and the Sub-Lieutenants as Lieutenants which seemed to straighten things out, particularly when army Adjutants acted as First Lieutenants on naval air stations.

There was a tendency for ex-naval officers to refer to the adjutants deprecatingly as 'those bloody soldiers' but this soon passed when they found that the soldiers, who took some pains to establish themselves and took care not to interfere with flying operations, were quite likeable men. Airship stations were particularly favourably placed as all airship operations and material remained under the Admiralty, only personnel belonging to the Royal Air Force. Airship Stations were still known as Royal Naval Airship Stations, although navy blue and khaki uniforms were mixed, ultimately merging into the pale Royal Air Force blue, which later became darker.

By the Commissioners for Executing the Office of Lord High Admiral of the United Kingdom of Great Britain and Ireland &c&c

George R.I.

To Mr. Thomas Blenheim Williams hereby appointed Flight Sub Lieutenant in His Majesty's Navy

By Virtue of the Power and Authority to us given by His Majesty's Letters Patent under the Great Seal We do hereby constitute and appoint you a Flight Sub Lieutenant in His Majesty's Navy Willing and requiring you to take upon you the Charge and Command of ... or the Charge and Command of any higher rank to which you may be promoted the same being notified to you by usual Gazette Strictly Charging and Commanding all the Officers and men of the Royal Naval Air Service subordinate to you to behave themselves jointly and severally in their respective Employments with all due Respect and Obedience unto you, and you likewise to observe and execute the General Printed Instructions and such Orders and Directions as you shall from time to time receive from us or any other your Superior Officers for His Majesty's Service Hereof nor you, nor any of you, may fail as you will answer the contrary at your Peril And for so doing this shall be your Commission. Given under our hands and the Seal of the Office of Admiralty this 7th day of ... 19.. in the ... Year of His Majesty's Reign.

By Command

With Seniority of ...

With effect while holding an appointment as an Officer of the Royal Naval Air Service.

George R.I.

George by the Grace of God of the United Kingdom of Great Britain and Ireland and of the British Dominions beyond the Seas King, Defender of the Faith, Emperor of India &c.

To Our Trusty and well beloved Thomas Blenheim Williams Greeting

We reposing especial Trust and Confidence in your Loyalty Courage and good Conduct do by these Presents Constitute and Appoint you to be an Officer in Our Royal Air Force from the First day of April 1918. You are therefore carefully and diligently to discharge your Duty as such in the Rank of Captain or in such higher Rank as We may from time to time hereafter be pleased to promote or appoint you to, of which a notification will be made in the London Gazette and you are at all times to exercise and well discipline in Arms both the inferior Officers and Men serving under you and use your best endeavours to keep them in good Order and Discipline. And We do hereby Command them to Obey you as their superior Officer and you to observe and follow such Orders and Directions as from time to time you shall receive from Us or any your superior Officer according to the Rules and Discipline of War in pursuance of the Trust hereby reposed in you.

Given at Our Court at Saint James's the First day of December 1918 in the Ninth Year of Our Reign.

By His Majesty's Command.

W.S. Brancker

W.A. Robinson

**T.B. Williams'
commissions into The
Royal Navy and Royal
Air Force.**

R 26 pictured with a towing tank, which saved considerable manpower.

Left: inside the keel of a rigid airship showing the walking way, the main passage way of early airships.

Right: a Sopwith Camel fitted to R23, July 1918. The walking way can be seen above the aeroplane.

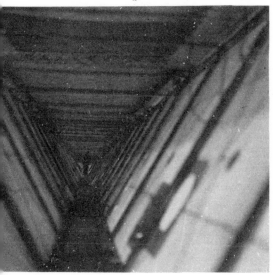

JSG.

ROYAL NAVAL AIR SERVICE.

AIRSHIP DAILY REPORT.

Llangefni, ANGLESEY................... Naval Airship Station.   Date 5th July 1918.

TOTAL PER PILOT.

Ship No. and Type.	Captain.	Time started.	Time returned.	Distance covered. Mls.	Object of Flight.
S.S.Z.34.	2nd.Lt.Brown.	0940.	1855.	200.	Patrol-trade route
S.S.Z.35.	Capt.Williams.	2120.	2235.	30.	Engine trial.
S.S.Z.50.	Lt.Carver.	0755.	1510.	160.	Patrol-trade & mail routes.
SS.Z.51.	2nd.Lt.Lamb.	0955.	1735.	195.	Patrol-trade route

TOTAL FLYING PER DAY.

Ship No.	Hours. Mins.		Miles.
S.S.Z.34.	9. 15.		200.
S.S.Z.35.	1. 15.		30.
S.S.Z.50.	7. 55.		160.
S.S.Z.51.	7. 40.		195.

flights by same ship to be added together and total given.

SHIPS READY TO FLY IMMEDIATELY.

Ship No.	Captain.	Ship No.	Captain.	Ship No.	Captain.
SSZ.34.	Lt.C.G.Wigglesworth.				
SSZ.50.	Lt.M.B.Carver.				
SSZ.51.	Capt.Campbell.				

SHIPS NOT READY TO FLY.

Ship No.	Cause.	What parts are required.	When demanded.	From whom demanded.
SSZ.35.	Changing Engine. (Carried out trials during day.) (Capt.T.B.Williams.)			

Sta. 8848/17.

[1515] 12085/D394 2m 6.17 1206 G & S 111

_____ Senior Flying Officer.

At Anglesey the only noticeable difference was the appointment of a khaki-clad executive officer to look after office work
and maintainance — a great help. I held off as long as possible but
the inevitable clash came when I had to accuse him of taking men
to wash windows when I needed them for a landing party.
Fortunately he saw my point of view and we had no more trouble;
flying always came first after this. I took the officer, Hazlett his
name was, for a local flight on 5th July when carrying out an
engine trial and the breach was sealed. This was my last flight at
Anglesey for I had had orders to join Captain Meager as his Chief
Officer to go out to Rome to fly home a semi-rigid airship bought
by the British Government from the Italians. My name appeared in
the 'Anglesey Airship Daily Report' as being discharged to the
Superintendant of Airships Department on 11th July. It was quite
a wrench leaving my SS-Zeros.

Opposite:
The daily Report for 5th July 1918 at Anglesey recording T.B. Williams' last
flight there.

D

Chapter 9

The first flight ever from Italy to England

In July, 1918 the crew for the Italian semi-rigid airship left for Rome. We travelled in an American troopship to Le Havre. I was interested in the mixture of discipline and otherwise displayed by the American soldiers. A smart salute for instance, coupled with addressing the officer by his christian name.

I found myself of sufficient rank to get a berth in a cabin, so I was able to get some sleep after we had left Southampton in convoy escorted by destroyers.

On arrival at Le Havre the airship crew was requisitioned by a brass-hatted army officer. In spite of my respectful protests we were handed rifles and given a party of deserters to escort to a barracks at the other end of the town. On delivering our unfortunate charges, I was given a receipt for their bodies and equipment. It was interesting to see batches of German prisoners being marched through the streets with one small French soldier carrying a very long rifle in charge. The Germans looked as if they had had enough and seemed glad of the chance of a bit of comparative comfort.

The train journey on to Rome was uneventful, although the passage through the Alps was particularly striking in contrast with the war conditions everywhere else, with a wonderful bright sky and the sun shining on the snow-covered peaks. A party of American nurses travelling with us were quite charmed with the sight, and we with them.

The leaning tower of Pisa was still leaning and the Italian skies a deep blue with the hot sun of mid-summer. We spent the night in Rome and transport arrived for us next morning to take us to our aerodrome at Ciampino, on 'the fever-stricken plain of Campagnia'. I found myself with a very pleasant room in the officers' quarters with the window overlooking the Appian Way. On the door was a card reading: *Capitano Williamo*.

The Captain of *SR-1*, George Meager, arrived a few days later with Major Cochrane and Flight Lieutenant Rope; the latter two officers, representing the Admiralty, were to examine and accept if satisfied the airship before the flying crew took her over for the flight to England. Later, in 1943, Cochrane then Air Chief Marshal Sir Ralph Cochrane, GBE, GCB, AFC, organized the raids on the Moehne and Eder dams, the success of which undoubtedly shortened the 1939-1945 war and saved many thousands of lives.

While waiting for the others to arrive I was able to get in a two hour flight to the Mediterranean on the trials of an Italian semi-rigid, called *O-1* which reminded me of my pet destroyer which worked with me in the Irish Sea *DO-1*. The *O-1* was piloted by the Commanding Officer of Ciampino, Major Biffi, and I believe that the airship was later sold to America.

There were some differences between the semi-rigids as built and operated by the Italians, and our own non-rigids and rigids. The rigids needed less pressure because their shape did not depend on the gas pressure, whereas the non-rigid depended entirely on sufficient pressure inside its envelope to keep the shape. The former had a low pressure of about 3 mm, but the non-rigid needed 25 mm when in flight. The semi-rigid came in between with 9 mm. The *SR-1* was a semi-rigid airship of half a million cubic feet capacity and of a type so far unused in England. She was claimed to be a high-flyer and a great weight-lifter, with a considerable length of flight potential.

The Italians seemed to land their airships faster than we did, despite the fact that they used swivelling bladed propellors, which acted as a brake and as a result they occasionally damaged members of the landing party. The aerodrome hospital was well stocked with malaria and accident cases.

We saw a nearly fatal example of this rapid style of operating when I was training at the Wormwood Scrubs Station early in 1916. We had a visit from a delegation from the Italian Airship

Service. The leader was a senior officer, very smartly dressed, and he was to be given a flight in a new type of SS built experimentally by Messrs. Armstrong Whitworth.

The Italian flying officer was offered a preliminary trip with a British pilot, but said that he was familiar with this type of airship and could manage very well. He handed us his beautiful cap and gold mounted cane and climbed on board while the mechanic swung the propeller to start the engine, after the ship had been ballasted up. In the meantime we young bloods stood by and heartlessly apportioned his belongings as mementos; I claimed the gold mounted stick which had been handed to me. We were soon shocked at our behaviour.

The ship took off at full throttle straight from the ground, swung to the right at full starboard rudder and struck the railings enclosing the aerodrome.

Our Engineer Officer, F.A. Baldwin, who was in the fore cockpit, was thrown out, luckily not very badly hurt. The fuselage was telescoped by the impact, the engine stopping fortunately at once. Some of the suspensions carried away and the shattered airship then ballooned up, with the pilot hanging head downwards pinned by his legs in the middle of the collapsed nacelle. The envelope appeared not to be much damaged and in any case the lower gas valve would blow at about 30 mm pressure so the ship would not travel far. Vehicles were hastily got out and the wreck was chased across London. It came down in Stepney, the envelope bridging across two rows of houses in a street. The poor battered body was lowered into waiting arms. I believe the pilot lived, but that he never flew again.

We learned about life from that.

To return to Italy and slow landing, the Italians seemed to be surprised at our method which we were able to demonstrate later; the landing party in particular approving of it.

We found on arrival that our *SR-1* — as the M-type semi-rigid for the British was to be called, was a long way from completion, so after a visit to the building hangar every morning and a close study of construction we would, whenever possible, hie us into

Rome or a nearby gracious place to enjoy the wonders and beauties available in the glorious Italian sunshine. There was a long siesta at midday, when I would 'collect' churches while others slept, that is visit as many as I could, comparing the architecture and decoration and atmosphere. In the evenings we would visit restaurants in Rome, particularly one run by old Francesco; or perhaps go to the Opera House.

The Italians in the streets treated us very well, often coming up to us and shaking us by the hand, or leaning out of cars to give us a cheer. Girls gave us hearty kisses on occasion, but not when their males were present. I enquired as to why we were so much more popular than the French, which fact was very obvious, and was told that recently when they were in difficulties on the Piave, the French had arrived and stated that 'We have come to save you' whereas the British had said: 'We have come to help you'. We tried to be equally modest.

I have mentioned that the window of my room at Ciampino overlooked the Appian Way, lined with the remains of old Roman tombs. At night the wine carts pulled by little horses, would rumble over the cobble stones, the driver often asleep. By the side of the highway ran the lines of a tramway-cum-railway. One night there was a commotion outside my window. A wine cart had wandered on the track and had been struck by a tram. The poor little horse was almost cut in half.

The water at Ciampino was undrinkable, so a carafe of wine at one's place at table was very welcome. I think that there is nothing more delicious than Italian wine. I remember the brands to this day. The proprietor of one of our favourite restaurants in Rome, old Francesco, told us one evening that he had secured a most wonderful bottle of wine for us. He opened it with great gusto and poured it as if it was something very precious. We tasted it. It was poor red French and very acid. We drank it, although with wry faces, to please Francesco!

Early we found that rough-house play was also indulged in by the Italian pilots. One flying officer came back from leave late one night to find all the furniture in his room piled high up on his bed.

I was shown this during the day and was asked to subscribe, so I crowned the pile with his jerry. He was in no mood to straighten his room when he arrived back and slept on the floor. This episode makes me think of the Dambusters organized by Air Chief Marshal Sir Ralph Cochrane, but the price we paid was the loss of nearly half of the Lancasters of No.617 squadron, with 56 aircrew lost of the total of 133. Wing Commander Guy Gibson, their leader, who survived, wrote personal letters to all the mothers of the dead fifty-six.

The full story is given by Paul Brickhill in *The Dam Busters* who also says:

> There are some who solemnly lament that wartime flying men were known on occasion to drink more than was seemly . . .
>
> Perhaps the rigidly virtuous might acquire a more flexible understanding if they followed the young pilot to the airfield and watched his face in its hood when the chocks were pulled away. Better still, follow him into the air, strapped to a seat and deafened by noise, held precariously aloft by wings relying on inconstant engines and petrol tanks, highly vulnerable to the assaults of flak and fighters, fog and ice-cloud. Follow him up there not once but sixty times till violent death is a threefold statistical certainty.
>
> They played hard because they had little time to play and more often than not it was high rather than potent spirits which affected them.*

The Italians would not let us go out on their bombing raids, made from Ferrara, or from Camp'alto near Venice. These bombardments were carried out on moonless nights usually by M Class airships, similar to our *SR-1*. The Austrian aeroplanes did not seem to go up and attack them, possibly because their bombing height was 13,000 to 14,000 feet; at which height the engines were only just audible from the ground.

Bomb loads in the 'Ms' was about half a ton with loads of

* *The Dam Busters* by Paul Brickhill: Evans Brothers. London 1951.

propaganda leaflets. The F-type would carry one and a half tons. Searchlights were switched on by the enemy, but the airships were seldom picked up. The ships always landed in the dark. An east wind was preferred so that the airship would drift homewards in case of trouble. On 30th September *M-14* cracked a cylinder when over the lines. The cylinder was changed in the air and the ship returned safely. This was quite a feat in the dark.

A system of prizes for officers taking part in bombing raids was in operation by the Italian Military Authorities augmented by other prizes donated by large firms. The officer who headed the list had carried out over fifty raids. During the year ending 18th August 1918, with four M-type ships, 109 bombardments were carried out, in which 70 tons of explosives and 20 tons of leaflets were dropped without casualties.

One fine day in August the Lord Mayor of London, Sir Charles Hensen, arrived at Ciampino and was given a flight over Rome in one of the Italian airships, to his great delight. F.M. Rope had a close relative who was an official in the Vatican and we were granted many privileges in consequence, such as escorted visits to remote parts of the catacombs which were still being excavated and several visits to the Vatican itself. The days passed and at last *SR-1* began to assume her final shape. The envelope was inflated and the two Itala-Maybach engines were installed, one on each side of the control car. In order to give us more speed, and to act as a reserve on our journey home, a third engine, a SPA, was erected on a gantry on the top of the control car, over our heads. Hammocks were slung from the keel in the open for sleeping purposes as there was no room in the control car.

On the 28th August *SR-1* was taken out of the hangar and with a crew of eight we were soon airborne and trials commenced. The trials were to include a height test as it was desired to use her for high bombing raids. The next day a further flight was made to test speed and climb.

On the 7th September a full speed trial was carried out. Various adjustments were necessary following this and a further flight was made on the 3rd October when particular attention was paid to engine and wireless performance.

On 12th October the acceptance flight was completed with a journey of 5½ hours from the mouth of the River Tiber to Ortebello. We spent up to midnight getting the airship ready for flight again.

We made a final visit to the Vatican and we were granted an audience by Pope Benedict XV, who blessed us and our airship, and wished us a safe journey home. I am not a Roman Catholic but went to Mass in St Peters' on one or two occasions with George Meager who is.

We kept the ship ready for flight, as instructions were received on the 14th that we should proceed to England as soon as weather conditions permitted. The British crew flew *SR-1* on the 20th for a two-hour local flight. In the evening I went into Rome to see Rope, just out of hospital with a fever. He was much better. Each day we made sure that the ship was at the last stage of readiness, but the weather had turned foul and the reports showed unsuitable conditions ahead. On the 23rd we carried out another two-hour local flight. We had some minor engine trouble, but altogether it was a very successful trip. We got up early each morning to study the weather reports. On the 25th we did a further flight to familiarize ourselves with the handling of the airship and to try out our slow landing technique while using the swivelling bladed propellers.

On the evening of 27th October 1918 the weather reports at last showed favourable conditions on our route, so the Italian flying officers gave us a grand dinner, as far as their rations would allow. Then, at 4.25 a.m. on the 28th October, we took off on the first flight ever from Italy to England.

The crew of *SR-1* comprised:

Captain	Captain G.F. Meager
Chief Officer	Captain T.B. Williams
Italian Officer	Lieutenant di Rossi
Coxswain	Chief Petty Officer G.F. Clarke
First Engineer	Chief Petty Officer R.G. Owen
Second Engineer	Petty Officer H. Leach

SR1 landing at
Ciampino, Rome, in
October 1918.

The car of SR1. The
sleeping berths, looking
like canoes, are hidden
under the envelope, but
the crew had no time
to use them on the
flight to England.

Major Cochrane doing
the tightrope walk on
the car of the SRI,
while examining.

Third Engineer   Petty Officer R. Tomlins
First Wireless Operator   Leading Mechanic B. Bocking
Second Wireless Operator   Air Mechanic R.J. Rook

As we left Rome before dawn and there were little or no lighting restrictions we had a glittering send-off. After some time we found that being surrounded by three engines, all running together, was absolutely deafening. The Spa started to give trouble very soon, developing leaks and plastering us with oil – to the detriment of our comfort and appearance.

We crossed the Italian coast at Lodispoli; off Civita Vecchia with a north-east wind we experienced heavy bumping from air currents over the mountains.

Elba was passed soon after eight o'clock in excellent weather, the wind veering further east helping our flight to Cape Corse and the south of France. We passed through a heavy rainstorm and then sighted the French coast at Antibes, and so uneventfully reached Marseilles, our flight taking just over 10½ hours.

On eaching the French Airship Station at Aubagne it was found to our consternation that the hangar was too small to take *SR-1* so the ship had to be moored out in the open between the shed windscreens. A considerable amount of gas had to be valved to get down at 3 p.m.; we had used 310 gallons of petrol. It took all hands working until midnight to take in a further 320 gallons of petrol, 17 gallons of oil and 350 tubes of hydrogen. No sleep could be taken as we were in the air again at 2.50 a.m. on the 29th, taking with us a French Airship pilot, Lieutenant Picard, to assist us over French territory. It must be remembered that there was a European War in progress and we had to follow a pre-determined route. It was always possible that we might be mistaken for a Zeppelin and shot down or up by the French.

We reached the River Rhone at Arles at 4.30 in the morning and followed it to Avignon and Montelimar, but the Mistral was blowing strongly from the north and our speed was reduced to about 20 knots, it taking us 2½ hours to reach Valence.

The ship was flown as closely to the ground as was safe, and at times French Army lorries travelling in the same direction were

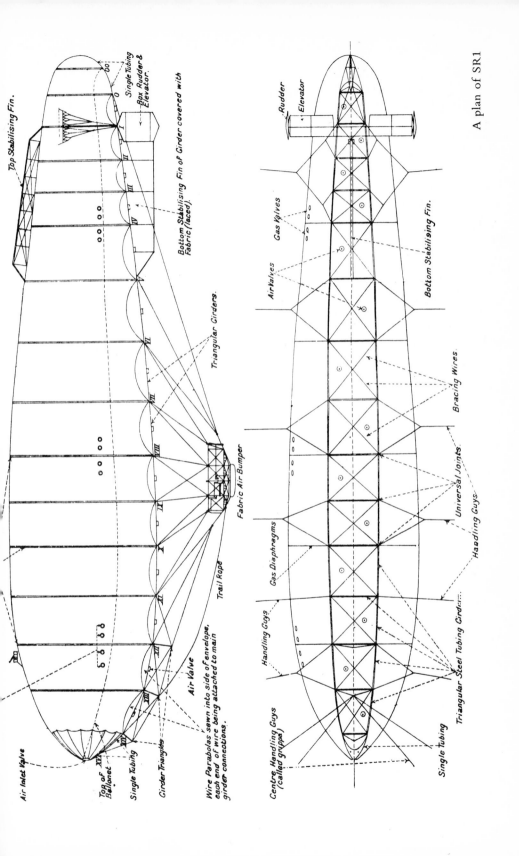

Top Stabilising Fin.

Single Tubing

Box Rudder &
Elevator.

Bottom Stabilising Fin of Girder covered with
Fabric (laced).

Triangular Girders.

Fabric Air Bumper.

Trail Rope

Air Inlet Valve

Air Valve

Wire Parabolas sewn into side of envelope,
each end of wire being attached to main
girder connections.

Top of
Ballonet

Single Tubing

Girder Triangles

Rudder

Elevator

Gas Valves

Air Valves

Bottom Stabilising Fin.

Bracing Wires.

Universal Joints.

Handling Guys.

Gas Diaphragms

Handling Guys

Centre Handling Guys
(called grippe)

Single Tubing

Triangular Steel Tubing Girder

A plan of SR1

catching us up and passing us. The frustration was frightful. It was twelve noon before we got to Lyon, but as the French weather report indicated a south-east wind outside the Rhone valley, it was decided to make a run towards Paris. At 1.30 the wind was still against us so the airship was turned about for Lyon and a landing made at the French emergency aeroplane landing ground at Bron at 2.50 p.m. We had been in the air for twelve hours. Here the ship was again tethered in the open, the mooring pennant being secured to a three-ton lorry filled with hydrogen cylinders and the guys made fast to screw pickets. Mercifully the wind fell completely and remained calm all night.

A lengthy delay was experienced here owing to the unfamiliarity of the men with airships; although they did their utmost, practically the whole work of gassing fell on the crew of *SR-1*, who had to instruct the French ground staff in handling the hydrogen tubes. There was only one twelve-way filler, and six of the junctions got blown out of their joints. 'By every one of the crew working like six men' (to quote the Flight Report), 300 tubes of hydrogen were put in and 430 gallons of petrol taken on board. The men were hard at it from the moment of landing till the time of leaving. The night was bitterly cold and everything was saturated with moisture.

Great difficulty was experienced in starting up the engines, but at 4.30 in the morning the Engineers got the two Italas running. At five o'clock, in miserably cold and wet conditions, we left the ground in thick mist, which we were told always lay over the Lyon district until about eleven o'clock. We broke part of the front of the control car in some trees in leaving, which exposed us still more to the unpleasant conditions.

SR-1 was ballasted up very light and rose to about 60 feet, then she commenced to fall. The starboard engine stopped because of the moisture and congealed oil and nearly all the water ballast had to be discharged to rise. Our only light was that from hand torches as it had not been possible to get our accumulators charged at Bron.

As soon as the mist cleared the ship became very light and

climbed. It was difficult to keep on an even keel with only one of our three engines running. The Spa engine overhead was finally got going about six o'clock and soon after we managed to start the other Itala.

Over the small town of Chauffailles part of the Spa exhaust pipe burnt through and broke off. Its surroundings were hundreds of gallons of high octane petrol and almost half a million cubic feet of very inflammable hydrogen. Why we were not immediately destroyed, I shall never know. The two of us nearest to a ladder leading to the top of the control car leaped for it. I think the other man was Leach. We threw the bits overboard and brushed off the sparks with our hands. When we got back into the control car I said to Leach: 'There is something wrong about that'.

'What is wrong, sir?' said Leach.

'We ought to be dead', I replied.

Fortunately the wind was now blowing strongly from the south-west, helping us considerably. At a quarter to eight we passed over Briare and from then until 8.20 the ground was blotted out by low lying clouds, when we reached the River Loire and followed it to Nevers.

A course was then set across wooded country to Montereau which we flew over at 12.25 midday. We then followed the River Seine to Paris, which we found bathed in thick mist, though we enjoyed a very close view of the upper part of the Eiffel Tower.

St Cyr Airship Station was reached at 3 p.m. where we were not expected; a wireless message had been sent instructing us to fly on to Le Havre, which had not been received. Hardly any wireless messages reached us over land; only over the sea could we get communication.

Another bitter pill awaited us on landing when we were told that the measurements given to us in July on the plan of the hangar were incorrect and that the shed was too small for SR-1 to get in. The ship was therefore once again refuelled and gassed in the open with its considerable difficulties, and danger from strong winds: 380 gallons of petrol had been used in the journey from Lyon, a flight of over 9 hours.

LANDED 14·40 — 6·11·1918
ARRIVED 13·30
CIRCLED WHILE R.23
DROPPED AEROPLANE
AND LANDED

Gt.Yarmouth

Pulham

12·30 Needham Market
11·30 Colchester   Harwich

ENGLAND   Southend 10·10
                      Kingsnorth
LONDON   Maidstone
LEFT 09·40   13·45
6·11·18
LANDED 14·15   Rye Bay
31·10·30
                  Hastings
          English Channel   12·45

                              Dieppe 11·00
          Fecamp   St.Valery-en-Caux 10·00
          9·15   Rouen 08·10
                   R.Seine   Les Andelys 07·50
          07·00 Mantes
LEFT: 06·15   St.Cyr   PARIS
31·10·18   Melun
LANDED: 14·00   Corbeil
30·10·18
                  12·25 Montargis
                              St.Fargeäu 10·45

          R.Loire   08·35 Nevers   Gueu

                       07·05 Chauffailles
                       Ambierle
                       TURNED
                       ABOUT 13·20
                                          Vier
          FRANCE
                              10·00 Vale
                              07·15 Montelin
                              06·30 Pont St.Esp
                              05·00 Av
                              04·30 A

          SPAIN

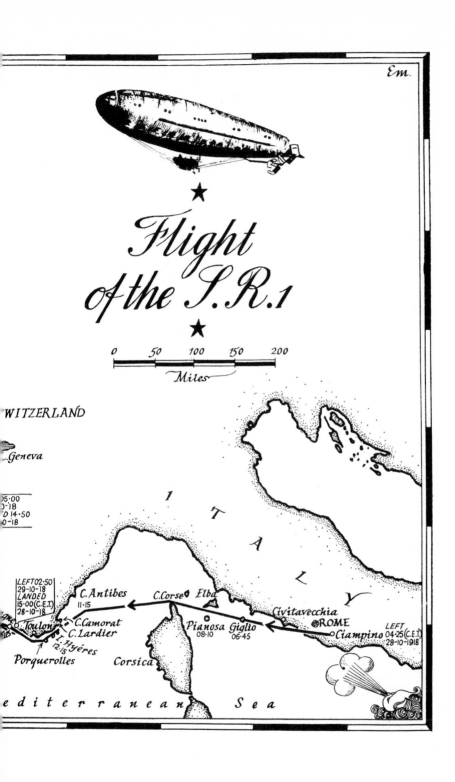

_Em._

★

Flight
of the S.R.1

★

0   50   100   150   200

Miles

WITZERLAND

Geneva

05·00
0-18
D 14·50
0-18

I
T
A
L
Y

LEFT 02·50
29-10-18
LANDED
15·00 (C.E.T.)
28-10-18

C. Antibes
11·15

C. Corse ◊ Elba

Civitavecchia
●ROME

Toulon
C. Camorat
C. Lardier
I. Hyéres
12·15

Pianosa   Giglio
08·10   06·45

Ciampino   LEFT 04·25 (C.E.T.)
28-10-1918

Porquerolles

Corsica

editerranean   Sea

Most of the crew had by now reached a state of semi-con-
sciousness. I remember it as a night of horror, trying to drive our
unwilling bodies to their tasks. It was a pitch black night and any
lights revealed us walking about as though drunk. I remember
returning to *SR-1* after a hasty meal in the officers' mess in the
night and tripping over a railway line beside the hangar, opening
up an old wound on my right shin bone. I can still feel the utter
agony of it and my efforts to appear nonchalant.

When I hear the name St Cyr, or French spoken in an excited
fashion, I recall hearing Lieutenant Picard, the French Airship
Officer who had escorted us from Marseilles, telling a group of
French pilots of the dreadful journey we had had and forecasting
disaster yet. We left him at St Cyr which gave us a little more
room for standing only in the oily mess, the cage that was politely
called our control car. All I prayed for at that time was for the
great Maybach-Itala engines to get going so that I could crouch
against one of the radiators to retain what little life was still left in
me.

We left St Cyr at 6.15 a.m. the next morning, after warnings of
a storm coming, and a suggestion that we could not be held in a
gale. We ran into a thick fog at 7.30 when flying over Andelys, and
soon after were flying in a heavy rain cloud at 300 metres. About
this time the hand on the low height aneroid broke off, but the
face was turned round completely and the blunt end used; it did
work, but it all added to our difficulties which had become legion.

Just before eight o'clock through a break in the fog we sighted a
large river running east and west, which we calculated was the
Seine to the south-east of Rouen.

Later when we estimated we should be over Rouen we
descended to 200 metres to get our bearings, but the clouds were
down to the ground which was completely out of sight.

I was at the height coxswain's post operating the elevators, and
was easing gently down through the fog to ascertain if we had
reached the coast. Very suddenly I saw some ground beside me,
part of a little hill, and on the top of the hill was a cow. We looked
straight into each other's faces: it was a brown and white cow of

the Ayrshire type. I don't know who was the most startled, the cow or I. The glimpse disappeared at once and still more gently I brought the nose of *SR-1* up, knowing that violent action would bring the tail of the airship down with possibly disastrous results. I held my breath. The cow did not appear again and I regained height safely.

Soon after nine o'clock we passed over the French coast, which we followed with difficulty as the fog was still thick. At ten o'clock a small port with two piers forming a harbour was reached, which was considered to be St Valery and at 10.15 we flew over Dieppe. After asking Polegate and Kingsnorth for weather reports without reply, we received a message from Capel Airship Station near Folkestone saying that they were covered with a thick mist.

When over the English Channel, we slowed down the engines to check the wind speed and direction and to gauge our buoyancy, but the Spa did not like it and blew out a plug, further anointing our devoted heads with hot, dirty oil. Having established wireless communication with Capel we passed all our messages through that station. At last Admiralty instructions were received to land at Kingsnorth and a course was sent for Chatham. The weather improved as we approached the English coast which we crossed over Rye Bay and at long last a landing was made at Kingsnorth at 2.15 p.m. after 8 hours in the air from Paris.

I believe that we attempted to start to refuel and regas to push on again, but we were gently restrained and persuaded that the first flight of an aircraft between Italy and England had been completed.

The crew of *SR-1* must have looked a dreadful sight when we landed. We were all deaf because of the roar of the three engines surrounding us, our eyes were bloodshot for want of sleep and due to the draught through the damaged bow of the control car, we were all filthy for need of washing, covered in oil from the Spa engine above, and gaunt from want of food and drink, and of course completely unshaven. There were many to greet us, but they looked at us in wonder, almost in fear. We must have looked like beings from another world. We could not bear to look at each other, and could scarcely believe that we had completed our allotted task.

As soon as *SR-1* was bedded down in one of the great hangars, we were led away like children and fed, then taken to quiet quarters that looked too clean for us. We were asleep in seconds and slept round the clock.

In no time it seemed, but really the next day, I was conscious of a voice speaking and saw a golden-haired cherub. I thought: 'Botticelli was right, angels do have golden hair. I knew that I would get killed on this flight'.

Then the cherub said: 'Your bath is ready, sir'.

While we had been away, the mess servants who had all been men, had been replaced by women!

SR-1 remained for some days at Kingsnorth while necessary repairs were carried out on ship and crew, before she flew on to her home base at Pulham Airship Experimental Station in Norfolk.

In December we had a 'Mention in despatches' from the Lord Commissioners of the Admiralty, transmitted to our station by the General Officer Commanding, Royal Air Force, which stated that 'they were of the opinion that the flight reflects very creditably both on the Captain and the Crew'.

Some day I must count up the number of engine stoppages, the mileage, the hydrogen and petrol consumption, the hours in the air, the hours of lost sleep and blood and tears; but I have a headache now simply from remembering the events of the flight. The Captain's Report ended with the words: 'Only by Providence was the ship got through'.

Chapter 10

Armistice

The next few days were occupied on the overhaul of *SR-1* but good material and workmanship were evident, and repairs were soon effected. The slung-up hammocks for sleeping in the open under the keel were taken down, unused: there had been no time to occupy them.

I went up to London to see my mother and my girlfriend, but had hardly arrived when a telegram came from George Meager recalling me, as General E.M. Maitland, the Superintendent of Airships, was on his way to see us. I just got back in time to hear our Chief say some very kind words.

On the evening of the 4th November, 1918, Meager and I were sitting in the lounge of the Officers' Mess at Kingsnorth when a messenger arrived and handed me a telegram. I opened it with some trepidation. It was sent from Anglesey and read:

Major Elmhurst sends his heartiest congratulations to Captain Williams on receipt of the Air Force Cross.

The next day another telegram arrived which said:

Please accept heartiest congratulations from all Officers on your well deserved honour: Airships, Llangefni.

Finally on the same date came a letter from General Maitland saying:

I am very pleased indeed to be able to congratulate you on your award of the Air Force Cross. It is satisfactory to see that your extremely good work has at last been recognized.

All the crew of *SR-1* later received decorations for the flight home, but I was missed out, I suppose because the date of my Air Force Cross synchronized with that of the flight.

On the 6th November at 9.30 a.m. *SR-1* again took to the air for her flight to Pulham Airship Experimental Station, her base, with Colonel Cunningham, a senior airship officer, as passenger; our Italian, Tenente di Rossi was still with us. An hour after we started the Spa engine stopped while changing over tanks but was soon restarted. Then the starboard Itala-Maybach began to give trouble and had to be switched off for examination. A carbon brush in the magneto was found to be sticking. This was cleared and the engine was started up again.

In spite of all this the Pulham Hangars were sighted at 1.15 when the starboard Itala failed yet again, but was restarted soon after. We had to wait until *R-23* was taken out; she was engaged in an aeroplane carrying flight, but we finally landed at 2.40 p.m. The next day *SR-1* made a local flight at Pulham carrying senior airship officers.

On 9th November, two days before the Armistice was signed, I travelled in *R-26* to the Lord Mayor's Show in London, probably the only time that an airship took part in this ancient ceremony.

It was about this time that George Meager and I were standing side by side on a very solemn parade before high-ranking officers.

I whispered out of the corner of my mouth to George: 'I could not find my Number-One jacket: do I look alright?'

'You look a bit scruffy', came the reply, 'but I have your jacket on!'

The 20th November was a red-letter day. *SR-1* acted as escort to the Fleet when the surrender of the German submarines was taken in the North Sea. With the white ensign flying above the German flag they were brought in to Harwich and tied up like great bunches of bananas — or so they appeared from the air – the official record, I believe, is that 176 were surrendered and a further 178 had been sunk during the war but perhaps I have muddled up the two World Wars. The next flight of *SR-1* was on the 7th December, 1918, when we took a party of naval officers

The surrender of a German submarine off Harwich,
20th November 1918.

Inside the control car of SR1, where the crew and
T.B. Williams watched the German submarines
surrendering.

over the North Sea to carry out some experimental work.

SR-1 was laid up for some time after this, and I was appointed Adjutant at Pulham and engaged in administrative work.

On 2nd July 1919, George Meager and I rejoined *SR-1* with our crew and flew to London to take part in the Peace Procession. As we were following the Heralds down the Mall both main engines suddenly stopped. We were over the Royal Landau when the roar of the engines ceased, but our experience and training had ensured that the ship was very light. She shot upwards into the clouds and rain, we feeling somewhat apprehensive as *R-33* was in flight above us, but our engines were soon restarted and we got clear. A return was made to Pulham where we landed at eight in the evening after a ten-hour flight.

In July an endurance flight was carried out with *SR-1*. We left the ground after dark on the 6th and landed at Pulham after dark on the 7th, the flight taking over 25 hours, and covering much of the West Country and Wales, where we distributed Victory Loan leaflets.

Most of the non-rigids had now been deflated, but *SR-1* was retained for some parachute experimental work, being deflated at the end of August 1919. During our parachute work, our second coxswain, a very light man, jumped from 2,000 feet on a very hot day, taking 4 minutes, 20 seconds to reach the ground.

The Registrar of the Central Council of the Orders of Knighthood summoned me to attend an investiture at Buckingham Palace on 2nd August, 1919 when His Majesty King George V pinned an Air Force Cross on my uniform. It was a great thrill to see my name in the Court Circular of that date. I had a terrible experience while marching up to the King as instructed. I slid on a mat and had a dreadful feeling that I would not recover. I ended up rather closer to His Majesty than I should have been. The King's startled look was immediately replaced by one of amusement. His very kind words were a great relief.

Flying was very soon suspended after this time. I was transferred temporarily to the Accountant Branch and was in charge of a group of stations for pay purposes, based on Pulham.

At last the heavy pressure of the war years was easing and we were able to enjoy some games and sports. I took up cross country running again and ran for my RAF group at Cambridge on several occasions.

Most of the war-time airship stations had now been closed, but Pulham, as the Airship Experimental Station, was retained. I was able to get a flight, in the one remaining experimental SS on 19th February, 1920, *SSE-3*.

I shared my time between *SR-1* and the Station accounting work.

Chapter 11

The first double crossing of the Atlantic by air

On Sunday, 13th July, 1919 our little band at Pulham had the thrill of landing *R-34* after flying a double crossing of the Atlantic between Great Britain and the USA; the first in history. The first single crossing had been made a month before by Alcock and Brown in a Vickers Vimy aeroplane from St Johns, Newfoundland, which town I was to know well in the near future, to a bay near Clifden in Ireland.

R-34 had previously completed a Baltic cruise of 2,400 miles, occupying 56 hours under adverse weather conditions. The airship was then taken over from the Admiralty by the Air Ministry and overhauled for the attempt on the Atlantic crossing. She left her base at East Fortune in Scotland early in the morning of Wednesday, 2nd July, and immediately disappeared into a low lying mist. On board in addition to her ordinary crew, 6 officers and 20 NCO's and men, was the Superintendent of Airships, General E.M. Maitland, and Commander L. Lansdowne, United States Navy.

The Captain of *R-34* was Major George Herbert Scott who had been our Commanding Officer at Anglesey and had left us in the autumn of 1916 to take over the first of our own rigids to fly, *R-9*.

R-34 was the second of the *R-33* Class. She was designed to work with the Fleet, but her first flight was not until March 1919 after the war was over, and she carried out some flying and mooring tests at the Pulham Mast, in addition to her double Atlantic crossing. She was 650 feet long, of about 2,000,000 cubic feet capacity and had five Sunbeam Maori engines. Her speed was about 60 knots.

On her Atlantic flight she carried sixteen tons of petrol, a ton of oil, three tons of water ballast and half a ton of drinking water; the total weight of supplies being over twenty-four tons.

Soon after 2 p.m. on the 2nd July she was over the Forth Bridge and left the north-east coast of Ireland three hours later, heading out over the Atlantic. The wind was from the east so one engine was stopped to conserve petrol. The speed over the sea was then about 57 miles an hour.

At 6 o'clock with the forward engine stopped, and the remaining four running at 1600 revolutions, the airship was flying between two layers of clouds in conditions similar to that found by Alcock and Brown on their recent east to west crossing which to them had almost proved fatal.

Breakfast at 7.30 consisted of cold ham and a hard boiled egg, bread and butter and hot tea; the water being heated by the exhaust of an engine. During the morning the wind still being favourable the two aft engines were stopped, but the ship maintained her speed with the two wing engines. Major Cooke the navigator, took observations from the top of the ship, *R-34* climbing sufficiently for his head to be above the cloud strata!

Lunch at 11.45 consisted of stew, potatoes, chocolate, and cold water. Wireless messages were received from East Fortune, the Air Ministry, HMS *Queen Elizabeth* and others.

In the afternoon a stowaway was discovered named Ballantyne, a member of the crew who had been left behind, but could not bear it. Unfortunately this action had robbed the ship of another 200 pounds of petrol. Later in the afternoon, another stowaway was found; a tabby cat this time, who spent her time eyeing the carrier pigeons!

Tea was served, comprising bread and butter and greengage jam, with two cups of hot tea and a little piece of cake. The First Officer of the ship lodged a complaint at lunchtime that someone had used a toothbrush to stir the mustard!

The wireless officer reported that he had received a message from St John's, but this was very faint. Beautiful rainbow effects were found in the clouds, one circling the ship and another encircling the shadow. In the late afternoon messages were received from the battle cruisers *Tiger* and *Renown*, but the sea had been invisible all day.

In the evening the clock was put back half an hour to correct Greenwich time. It was calculated that *R-34* had covered 610 sea miles in 17 hours, an average speed of 36 knots. At 7 o'clock the airship was driving through heavy wet clouds and became very heavy. All engines were increased to 1800 revolutions to maintain height with the ship 12 degrees down by the stern. A glimpse of the sea was obtained through a gap in the clouds.

After a supper of hot cocoa, the watch off duty took to their hammocks in the keel, using extreme care in doing so. If one fell out it was possible to break through the lower outer fabric of the ship with the next stop the Atlantic some 1,500 feet below.

The weather improved by noon the next day, but the wind was increasing and by the evening was blowing from the south-south-east at about 45 knots decreasing the ship's speed. During the afternoon the starboard midship engine developed a crack in a cylinder water jacket but the Chief Engineer made a quick repair with copper sheeting and the ship's entire supply of chewing gum, which had to be chewed by three engineers before use.

Very rough weather was experienced in the evening with torrents of rain, but the airship rode well. The Meteorological Officer unfortunately shut his hand in the wireless cabin door, but his injury was not serious, although it was considered that his flow of language may have had something to do with the stormy conditions.

In the late evening the weather improved and the moon was seen rising in a clearer sky.

At dawn of the third day, Friday, 4th July, the lower sky colours were of lovely pastel shades, with a bright blue sky above a thin fog below, obscuring the sea. Later the fog cleared and an enormous iceberg became visible, with another in the distance, which were the only objects that had been seen on the flight so far.

Just before two o'clock a few small, rocky islands were

observed and the ship's course was altered slightly accordingly. Eventually the coast of Newfoundland was crossed at Trinity Bay in thick fog at 1,500 feet. The time taken between Ireland and Newfoundland was 59 hours. Over Newfoundland the fog cleared inland, the ship passing out over Fortune Harbour and the islands of Miquelon and St Pierre. When I was in Newfoundland later I was told that it was a Newfoundlander's sport to land on St Pierre on a dark night to steal the much-coveted boots from French fishermen's feet. Perhaps just a story.

In the evening the tramp steamer *Seal* was sighted bound for Sydney, Nova Scotia, the first ship seen. At 8.15 p.m. the northern point of Cape Breton Island was sighted with the distinctive four flashes from the lighthouse.

The night was very dark but clear, with the lights of White Haven showing brightly on the starboard side and the lights of a steamer passing to the east. There were strong headwinds, and *R-34* was making no appreciable headway. In the afternoon heavy squalls were encountered and Scott turned inland in an effort to avoid the wind blowing up the coast. Endless forest land was flown over, the scent of the pines reaching up to the ship.

Concern was now growing as to the stock of petrol and the engineer officer, Lieutenant J.D. Shotter, was busy checking up on the available quantity in the tanks when a squall hit the ship throwing down the nose. Shotter was crawling beside the drogue hatch and would have slid into the sea but he was just able to hook his foot into a girder in time.

There was still 500 miles to fly to reach New York and Commander Lansdowne sent a message asking for a destroyer to be sent to take *R-34* in tow in case the petrol supply gave out.

Severe storms were observed along the Canadian Coast and Scott turned towards the east to avoid them. Early in the evening the weather cleared and the ship was headed straight for New York.

Another storm was met during the night but at 4 a.m. the following morning, 6th July, the American coast was reached at Chatham.

It was decided not to fly over New York before landing owing to the shortage of petrol, and soon after midday the landing ground at Mineola was reached. Captain Pritchard parachuted onto the landing ground to assist the landing party and at 1.54 p.m. Greenwich time, 9.54 a.m. United States summer time, the ship was landed. She had flown 3,200 miles in 108 hours 12 minutes. Pritchard had become the first man to cross the Atlantic by air from east to west.

A great welcome awaited the airship and during the three days stay, the crew was overwhelmed with hospitality.

During the stay in New York one of the carrier pigeons escaped, and later landed on the deck of a steamer 800 miles out, dead on course for England!

Just before midnight on 9th July R-34 left Mineola and flew over New York. At midnight the miles of brilliant lights made a striking sight. The ship flew over Fifth Avenue, Times Square and Broadway and the crew could distinctly see thousands of upturned faces. Then a course was set for home, with a following wind and 3,000 miles to fly.

Soon after 2 a.m. on the 10th the American coast was crossed with four out of the five engines running, the fifth resting.

At 9.15 the airship had already covered 430 miles from New York and was 'going strong'. The mails were sorted and it was found that there was a large collection, including some for His Majesty the King, the Foreign Office, the Admiralty, the Postmaster General, and copies of the 'Public Ledger' for the Editor of The Times, which proved to be the fastest newspaper delivery between New York and London yet accomplished.

The ship was now making 72 knots, or 83 miles per hour on four engines. Lunch at noon comprised cold Bologna sausage and pickles and stewed pineapple. A ration of rum was issued as the weather had turned much colder. The ship was flying as steady as a rock, although it appeared from the air that a very heavy sea was running. The weather was clear and the navigator was able to get some very good observations.

Early the next morning, the 11th, the foremost of the two

engines in the aft car broke down, the bolts had sheared on the connecting rods and so badly damaged the crankcase that the engine was beyond repair.

At 8 o'clock heavy cloud on the port beam indicated bad weather conditions over Newfoundland. At noon a weather report was received from the Air Ministry and the course changed to take advantage of the expected westerly wind. The Air Ministry also stated that destroyers were available off Ireland if necessary.

The weather was very cloudy all this day and no observations could be taken, but a wireless message was picked up from HMS *Cumberland*, range 30 miles, giving her position. There was very heavy rain in the evening and throughout the night; that evening also the airship received a position from SS *Dominion*. At daybreak the next day, Saturday, 12th July, the weather was clearer, the sea being visible from 2,500 feet and the sun appeared in a blaze of colour. At 6 a.m. the ship was running on three engines, the remaining aft engine having broken down. HMS *Tiger* gave her position at 8 a.m. and gave the wind speed and direction as north-westerly, 15-20 mph. The breakfast was ample that morning and a good lunch was served. At 5.30 p.m. two trawlers were sighted on the starboard bow and at 7 o'clock a bearing was obtained on Clifden by directional wireless and at 8 p.m. the Irish

Major G.H. Scott reads George V's message after landing *R-34* at Pulham.

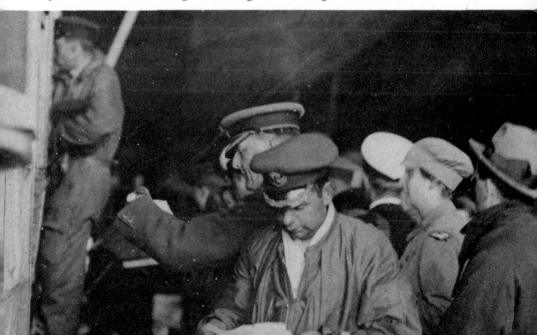

coast was crossed. Later a message was received from the Air Ministry that *R-34* was to land at Pulham, and her course was altered accordingly.

At dawn on the 13th July, all those available were in attendance on the aerodrome at Pulham. At last the beautiful silver shape of *R-34* was sighted and she made a circuit. She was landed by a handling party without difficulty. We soon had Scott with us again, and reading a congratulatory telegram from the King. The ship was safely housed in a hangar by seven o'clock. The first double crossing of the Atlantic by air had been completed successfully!

William Ballantyne, the stowaway, was left behind in the United States to return home by sea. On his arrival back he was dismissed from the crew of *R-34*, but was later posted to the crew of *R-80*; there was no court martial. Ballantyne found that the disapproval of Scott in particular, and of the members of the crew generally, coupled with dismissal from the ship, was punishment enough. He said that a large sign on the roof of a building in New York was no consolation: 'Ballantyne's Beer is Best' it read.

R-34's time for the return journey from Long Island to Pulham, Norfolk, was 75 hours, 3 minutes, giving a total time in the air of 183 hours for the flight in both directions.

I carried on with my accounting work at Pulham until April 1920 with a rapidly decreasing population.

I had applied previously for a permanent commission, but changed my mind and asked for the application to be cancelled. While I was in Newfoundland later I had an offer of a commission in the Accountancy Branch of the Royal Air Force, but felt that I could not face watching other men fly.

My turn for demobilization came when I was one of the last left. I felt relief at first being out of harness, but soon I regretted my request to cancel my application for a permanent commission: I missed the active life and the fascination of flying airships — although the actual flying decreased rapidly on the signing of the Armistice. I was at a loose end for some months, but expect that the rest did me good.

Chapter 12

The Newfoundland Airship Expedition

In the middle of 1920 I saw an advertisement in the *Daily Telegraph* asking for airship crews. I replied immediately and was eventually appointed as the Senior Pilot of an airship expedition being fitted out to go to Newfoundland, first to work with the seal fishery and later to develop aerial survey work. Four SS airships had been presented for the purpose by the Air Ministry to the Newfoundland Government with 50% spares, sheds, workshops and transport.

The organizer – Frank Tippen – and I soon became close friends and together got down to details. The operating company was The Aircraft Manufacturing Company of Canada whose Managing Director was Major K.E. Clayton-Kennedy. I agreed a contract with the Aircraft Manufacturing Company on 9th October, 1920.

I at once got busy getting our equipment together at a wharf at Purfleet, including visits to Wormwood Scrubs, my first Service Station. On 29th October we sailed from the Thames in the SS *Alconda* with all our material loaded in the holds. With the exception of two ladies, the wife of a paperworker at Grand Falls and her sister, Frank Tippen and I were the only passengers. The two ladies retired to their cabin on arrival and we scarcely saw them again until the end of our voyage.

The remainder of our personnel, whom Tippen had engaged in London, were to come out on the SS *Digby* from Liverpool on the 5th November. Also on this later journey came Sidney Cotton, an aeroplane pilot and the inventor of the *Sidcot* flying suit, David Plaistowe as second aeroplane pilot and two mechanics.

On the day we sailed there was a long account of the

Expedition in *The Times* and it was mentioned in several other newspapers. I heard later that the information had been supplied by Frank Tippen, and that Clayton-Kennedy was furious at this publicity appearing without his sanction as Tippen's employer.

On Sunday, 7th November we had a very bad storm. The violent movements of the steamer caused some of our cargo in the holds to move, in particular a workshop lorry broke adrift and had to be lassoed – which was only achieved at considerable risk of injury to members of the ship's crew. Tippen and I lashed ourselves to bolted down chairs in the small saloon, trying to appear nonchalant. During a slight pause in the antics of the ship, the door of the galley burst open and a shower of china fell to the floor; a lone saucer travelled down the passage and came to rest at my feet. During the evening of the 9th we sighted two large icebergs; and later a number of growlers – as small icebergs are called. At seven in the evening we saw the light on Fogo Island on the north coast of Newfoundland.

At daybreak the next morning we altered course for the mouth of the River of Exploits and soon after picked up a pilot who put off from amongst the rocks in a tiny motor boat. Slowly we passed up the river to a row of wharves, used by the Anglo-Newfoundland Development Company's paper mills at Grand Falls. The wharves were fully occupied so we dropped anchor in the river and the four passengers, the two ladies for Grand Falls and Tippen and I, went ashore at midday by the little tugboat *Exploits*. We landed by scrambling over a schooner loading lumber and were at last in Botwood, our destination.

My first impression was anything but favourable. The desolate stump-strewn soil with the scattered frame dwellings was anything but picturesque and the heavy rain that commenced to fall hardly improved the uninviting winter's day in a northern clime.

Tippen and I first went to the Staff House of the Anglo-Newfoundland Development Company to secure quarters there if possible, but were met with a response of 'No room', so we went to the office of the Anglo-Newfoundland Development Company and saw one Jones, who escorted us to a gaunt establishment named the Argyle Hotel. Here we left our impedimenta and began our search for an aerodrome site. Within a few days we had fixed on a spot near Botwood called Peter's Arm. On the 12th Clayton-Kennedy, came to see us, arriving at 6.30 p.m. and leaving at 7.45 p.m. by a specially chartered motor boat across the river to catch the so-called 'Express' train from the station at Norris Arm to the capital of St. John's.

During the night there was a heavy fall of snow, much deepening the coating lying there already and we awoke to find a world entirely black and white. On the 13th the *Alconda* came alongside the wharf, and we started unloading on the 15th November. The material was stored in one of the Anglo-Newfoundland Development Company's paper sheds. In the evening I had supper with the local JP whose appearance was of that of a typical Thames bargee.

The SS *Digby* had reached St. John's the previous day with our mechanics, McCoan and Cross, Speed, the hydrogen man; Skelton, shed constructor; and Heath, wireless. They reached us on the 17th with the aeroplane party: Captains Cotton and Plaistowe — the former I had already met in a recent Aerial Derby — and a mechanic called Cleaver. Wallace, the remaining member of the team, arrived a little later.

The Crossley tender from our cargo was started up and caused considerable excitement as it was the first motor vehicle of its kind seen in the settlement. Unfortunately the frost had damaged the radiator of the lorry we had brought but it could be used. Sidney Cotton had to go to Montreal, leaving Plaistowe in charge of the aeroplane contingent.

The cold was terrible, at night time particularly, and we suffered in our frame hotel. I had to wrap myself in spare suits of underclothing, and later took to sleeping in my flying suit. I was warned by a doctor I met in the post office to keep my ears covered as I had a slight touch of frostbite. Soon, however, we were fortunate in being able to rent Falkenburg House, which belonged to a wealthy timber owner, who was wisely away in warmer climes.

E

A telegram arrived on 20th November from the Seal Fishery Companies in St. Johns asking for details of progress and in the evening of the 22nd Brian Dunfield, a Director of Job Brothers, the seal fishery company arrived. Local labour had been engaged and parts of the hangar were being taken to the site we had selected at Peters Arm for erection.

The following day the Crossley tender was twice stuck in snow drifts, which of course caused delay. An earlier start was made the next day and the clearing of the ground for the shed was commenced. It was only then that we began to realize the magnitude of our task.

Ice-breakers showed great activity in smashing the ice round the *Alconda* and she duly sailed on the 25th. The same day the *Cranley* arrived bringing Wallace, the aeroplane engineer, and some more airship and aeroplane material. In the evening we skated on the frozen River of Exploits, under ideal conditions, a full moon and perfect ice.

During the next few days I got out a system of accounts and took photographs of our work in progress in clearing the ground and erecting the hangar.

More snow fell on the 28th. On that day Tippen and Plaistowe left on a rail pump cart, worked by two men with levers, for the main railway at Bishop Falls to catch the Reid train to St. Johns. McCoan and Cross worked the handcart and returned half frozen, with icicles on their noses and mouth.

Then events started to happen in rapid succession. A cook arrived from St. John's, and also a letter from Clayton-Kennedy in Montreal with considerable detailed instructions, including a demand for at least one airship 'to take away' by February; however, he did also include a cheque for $1000. Another letter was from the Minister of Agriculture and Mines stating that the airships had been placed in charge of his Department. A further letter was from the Newfoundland Colonial Secretary saying that the Government was not disposed to buy a set of meteorological instruments for our use.

Evidence that there was considerable friction building up

between the various interested parties rapidly showed itself as on 1st December the Anglo-Newfoundland Development Company impounded the material being stored in their paper sheds because of the non-payment of freight and local charges. The *Alconda* belonged to them. We could not remove any further material for a time, but busied ourselves with erecting hangar parts already on the site. On the same day ice-breakers cleared a track for the *Cranley* to get out to sea.

The following day I took the precious draft with me and boarded a coach attached to the local paper train en route for Grand Falls where I joined Tippen at Cabot House, the local hotel. He had another draft for $500 and we deposited our holdings at the local bank. Then I returned to Botwood with Tippen and found that the Government had arranged with Anglo-Newfoundland Development Company to release our material.

The cold grew worse day by day and work in the open became more and more difficult. No metal could be touched with bare hands and much snow fell. Work in the open was an agony. Soon we had a strike on our hands for more pay for the local labourers, the first deputation reaching us before breakfast on 7th December and at the same time we had the news that the wife of our 'shed erector' who had come out here with him, had given birth in the night to a dead baby.

Tippen called together the airship staff and admitted that circumstances generally were far from good, which was only too evident, and went on to explain that we were forced to reduce our labour force and must depend more on staff assistance. The 'shed erector' had proved pretty hopeless anyway, not being at all clear as to how the first frame should be erected.

On December 10th a telegram arrived from the Seal Fishery Companies in St. John's asking Tippen and me to meet them in the city. Cotton had arrived there and Plaistowe was with him. We delayed a day to make arrangements for the work to proceed and then found we had reached Sunday with no means of reaching the railway main line at Bishop's Falls.

Tippen and I, ignorant of the conditions and 'bloody minded', said that we would walk it, a distance of ten miles along a narrow gauge branch railway track! We loaded our luggage on our backs and set out, arriving at our destination with a blizzard behind us, just before dark and realized what a risk we had taken. We were glad to take refuge in a little frame hotel, where we played many games of chess with the local inhabitants. Some rest, then at 2.30 a.m. another mile to the railway station, where at about 3 o'clock a pair of great engines arrived towing the 'Express' along the three foot six inch track. Fortunately we found two sleeping berths available. These were held open by strong steel cables, which we were told were necessary to ensure that the occupants were not trapped inside should the train jump the track. This actually happened to me on a train I was travelling in on a later journey.

We reached St. John's the next day and retreated to the Cochrane Hotel, which at that time was an establishment with the convenience and comfort of a boarding house in the Euston Road and the daily charge of the Ritz but we were guests of the Government. We were greeted by the inhabitants with copies of a local newspaper with headlines such as 'The Airship Situation' and 'Here's a how-di-do'.

The next day we visited Job Brothers, the Chief Seal Fishery Company, who were very concerned about the situation in general.

Some days were spent in visiting various Government Departments. These visits included meeting an invitation to the house of the ex-Minister of Militia, and at his request the Minister of Marine and Fisheries who was on his way to a Cabinet Meeting. The Minister of Agriculture and Mines, who had informed us that the airships were in his charge and who was known amongst us as the Air Minister, eventually arranged a meeting for us with the Prime Minister of Newfoundland, Sir Richard Squires, which was extremely long and involved.

It was evident that the Prime Minister was as lost as everybody else and eventually announced that he would arrange a Government Conference.

A Martynside plane, 'Pixie B' towing boat and a dog team crossing the ice in Hawke's Bay, Newfoundland.

We waited for days for some movement and were then told that the Air Minister was going 'to the woods' to investigate and we had the pleasure of seeing him off at the railway station. A day or two later the Prime Minister sent for me and told me to return to Botwood to look after the airships; Sidney Cotton and I left St. John's together on 30th December, arriving at Grand Falls more or less on time, 36 hours later.

The winter conditions were often so severe that snow drifts held up transit for weeks on end. On my later visit to Newfoundland a train I was waiting for was about a month late; when I was nearly suffocated by a coke stove in the cabin of a motor boat in which I was waiting.

At Grand Falls there was a telegram from the Minister for Air asking me to wait there to meet him on his way through from Botwood. He gave me definite orders to cease all operations until he was able to discuss matters with other members of the Cabinet. The meeting was held at Lord Northcliffe's house, where the Minister stayed the night. We had to stay also as we had missed the train for Botwood. Plaistowe turned up on a locomotive and travelled to Botwood with Cotton and me the next day.

Tippen sent me a telegram saying that a heavy conference was in progress in St. John's and two days later I had a long personal telegram from the Prime Minister saying in effect that they were not responsible for anything. Cotton left the same day for St. John's to size up the situation as far as he was concerned.

It seemed obvious to me that the whole project had fallen down and I informed the staff accordingly. Living conditions were dreadful: we were short of cash, of food, of fuel, in a temperature often down at night in the region of 30°F. below zero. We would take hand sleighs into the woods to collect fuel for our big Swedish stove, which had an enormous appetite.

On 14th February I received a telegram from Tippen in St. John's to join him with the airship crew and personal gear. We travelled at the first available opportunity and arrived in St. John's in bitter weather on the 23rd. I arrived late in the evening out of funds at the moment and seeing a light in the Prime Minister's Office called on him and borrowed twenty dollars, which was refunded by Tippen later.

Tippen and I stayed in the Cochrane Hotel as Government guests until 10th March, when I boarded the SS *Sable Isle* with three members of our crew. Heath, the wireless operator, had joined Sidney Cotton. We transferred to the RMS *Saxonia* at Halifax bound for England. It was a bitter disappointment.

The position could not be better described I think, than by quoting from Sidney Cotton's autobiography:*

Clayton-Kennedy's plans were probably too extravagant; anyway he was in financial difficulties. His contract provided for a single payment from the sealing companies of 50,000 dollars at the start of the season, and on the strength of this he had secured a Bank overdraft. But the overdraft was mounting, the Banks were getting concerned and all Clayton-Kennedy's efforts to get a bigger payment out of the sealing companies failed. Negotiations continued for the whole of December and most of January, while preparations at Botwood stood still.

The whole operation turned very much on the question of confidence, since the sealing companies, like ourselves, had been told again and again that they were on to a madcap

* *Aviator Extraordinary*; the Sidney Cotton Story as told to Ralph Barker (Chatto & Windus, 1969).

scheme. Eventually the companies revoked the contract, and the Bank then gave Clayton-Kennedy three days to clear his overdraft. Since he had borrowed the money against the contract he hadn't a hope of repaying it.

All our personal contracts foundered if Clayton-Kennedy went under; and in any case I was most reluctant to see the expedition fail before it had had a chance to prove itself. I therefore offered to take over the contract – if the sealers would give it to me – and pay off the overdraft provided all the existing equipment was turned over to me. Clayton-Kennedy accepted and the Bank, who had no hope of getting any of their money back except by selling off the equipment, which nobody else wanted, agreed, though the sealers took the opportunity to knock down the sum payable under the contract from 50,000 to 40,000 dollars. As Clayton-Kennedy's overdraft was already 26,000 there wasn't much left, but I was prepared to lose money in the hope that we'd make a success of it and that the sealing companies would take up the option they had for the following year.

As soon as I got control I dispensed with the airship party, though I kept on a radio operator named Heath; and the following year Williams, the airship pilot, returned to work with me.

I rejoined Sidney Cotton in February, 1923 and a certain amount of aeroplane work was done, but the appalling weather conditions were prohibitive and eventually Cotton pulled out and went to the United States and I sent on his aeroplanes by sea.

The *Daily Express* of 9th July 1921 gave an account of how Cotton tried to meet the needs of the Sealing Industry but was finally beaten by the conditions.

In 1921 Botwood was used by aeroplanes carrying mail to Canada and much later, in 1939, it saw the inaugural flight across the Atlantic to England of Pan American Airways commercial service followed by Imperial Airways first Atlantic flight from Botwood to Ireland in the same year.

Chapter 13

Civil Airships at Pulham

Soon after I returned to England in 1921, following the abortive attempt to fly airships in Newfoundland, I was appointed by the Controller General of Civil Aviation as a Civil Airship Officer — I was the second to be appointed, the first being Scott — and posted for duty at Pulham Airship Experimental Station, which I had left not so many months previously. I was to serve with Major George Herbert Scott on airship mooring mast work, which suited me excellently.

Scott was our leading airship pilot. He was the Captain of the first rigid to fly, No.9, and in charge of R-34 on her double flight of the Atlantic in 1919. He was later killed in an airship when R-101 was lost.

Following her record flight, R-34 did not fly again until February, 1920. She began training work in January 1921, but was badly damaged that same month, and it was decided to delete her. The torch was then carried by R-33, her sister ship, both being designed on the lines of the German Zeppelin L-33. These two ships were post war deliveries, as their first flights were in March, 1919; R-33 was built by Armstrong Whitworth at Barlow and R-34 by Beardmore at Inchinnon. They were the first really useful British rigids, although their speed in practice was about 50 knots against a theoretical 60.

R-33 began mooring trials at the Pulham mast, which was fitted at the top with the Bedford-Pulham attachment constructed at Cardington, in February 1921, flying from Howden to Pulham.

This was the system of handling. A wire cable was threaded through a female inverted cone fitted to an upward projection at the top of a tall lattice-work steel mast. There was a winch at the lower end of the mast, to which one end of the wire cable was attached. The end of the wire passing through the attachment at the top, was carried out to a point on the aerodrome marked with a flag.

The airship carried a male inverted cone hanging from the tip of the bow, through which a similar wire cable was passed.

At the end of the wire from the mast which was taken to the flag, and at the end of the airship's wire, were the two halves of a quick-coupling device.

When a ship was coming in to land it came in at a low altitude and at a slow speed. On reaching the vicinity of the flag the wire of the airship would be dropped, and a man standing in attendance would quickly couple the ends of the two wires together. He had to be careful to be sure that the airship wire touched the ground before he handled it in order to discharge any static electricity picked up by the airship in flight.

The ship, which had been ballasted up slightly light in buoyancy, would then gently rise, and the winch would slowly take in the slack of the wire until it became taut, and then haul in on the coupled wires which were running through the attachments at the mast-head and the ship's bow.

When the ship's bow was close to the mast-head, the cone of the ship was drawn very slowly into the cone of the mast and automatically locked.

The mast-head attachment was free to revolve so that the ship, while floating at the head of the mast, was able to turn with it's bow always into the wind.

A vast amount of experience was obtained with *R-33*, about 50 mast landings being carried out up to 11th June, when she was taken into the hangar for overhaul. She held the record of 800 hours in the air. In July she carried out a flight of 31 hours covering many of the cities of England and Wales in connection with Victory Bonds, as *SR-1* had done a year previously.

R-33 had a very varied career, including carrying aloft fighter aeroplanes and dropping them off in flight; checking the night lighting of the London-Paris route; carrying police to observe

R33 returning to Pulham after breaking away from her moorings.

The new nose for R33 being hoisted into position at Pulham, August 1925.

Epsom Race traffic; and making a visit to the Hendon Air Show which was becoming a spectacle of considerable public interest. R-33 had given ample proof of the practicability and value of the airship mooring mast, not more than a dozen men being required for handling, and airships being able to operate in thirty-five knot winds.

It was a fascinating sight when by day or by night, repair and maintenance were carried out on the airship moored on the mast head. With flood lights at night and the activities of the flight and ground crews there was some flavour of a naval dockyard.

On the 15th April, R-33 was riding out a very strong gale with extraordinarily violent gusts when the ship broke away from the mooring, tearing the outer cover and deflating the forward gas bag. An 'anchor watch' crew was on board at the time. An examination showed that the bow was completely smashed in, and the deflated gas bag was lashed to frame No.2 to form a bulkhead to prevent further damage. The airship was being carried east with the wind, but in half an hour all the engines were running slowly, the ship still drifting at 30 miles an hour, at 2,000 feet.

R-33 was driven out over the North Sea with HMS *Godetia* and a destroyer from Lowestoft following. The airspeed had to be kept low as it was feared that the temporary bulkhead would not stand the pressure at high speed. The ship was driven astern over the Dutch coast during the evening, but during the night some headway was made as the 50 mile an hour wind abated. Slow headway was made after a further fall in the wind and in the middle of the afternoon of the 17th she reached Pulham and was landed.

During October 1925, R-33, now fitted with a new bow specially strengthened for mooring, carried out further experiments at the mast, including the carrying of Gloster Grebe fighter aeroplanes which were dropped off or attached in flight. Experimental flights were also carried out with a DH-53 with considerable success.

This great airship was not dismantled until 1928.

R-35, of Admiralty design and in general conforming to

Zeppelin practice, was begun at Armstrong Whitworth's works at
Barlow in the middle of 1918 but was slowed down at Armistice
time and cancelled early in 1919, her parts being used for *R-36*,
which was a lengthened *R-35* Class airship, based on Zeppelin
L-48. She was to have a 17,000 feet ceiling with a capacity of
2,101,000 cubic feet. *R-36* had been laid down at Beardmore's
before the Armistice, but was suspended then. It was later decided
to complete her as a civil airship. A greatly increased lift was
obtained by a considerable lightening of the structure. The
principle innovation in her design was the provision of accommo-
dation for 50 passengers with two-bunk cabins, toilets and galley.

   R-36 first flew on 1st April, 1921, the third birthday of the
Royal Air Force. The following day she left for Pulham and
landed to a handling party. She was then walked over to the mast,
the two mooring wires attached, the ship let up and then secured
in the normal way, with her male cone entering the female cone of
the mast.

   A few days later she left, with Scott in command, on her
demonstration and acceptance flight when the upper vertical and
starboard elevator fins collapsed while flying in bumpy conditions.
The ship took up an angle of about 35° down by the bow. The
engines were slowed down and water ballast from the bow was
dropped to adjust the inclination. The ship rose to about 4,300
feet; by this time the trim had been adjusted by moving the crew
in the keel. Engine speeds were adjusted to counterbalance the loss
of plane surface control. Two of the crew gallantly secured the
broken fins and the ship returned to Pulham where a night landing
was made, the vertical control being almost entirely achieved by
the movement of the crew along the keel.

   In the meantime *R-33* had been taken out and attached to the
mast to make room for *R-36*; much of the available space was
taken up by the two Zeppelins *L-64* and *L-71* surrendered to the
British at the end of the 1914-1918 War.

   In June a flight was made to Ascot with *R-36* carrying members
of the Press. Some complained that they could not see very well
and that food was conspicuous by its absence, but agreed that it

was more comfortable than the Great Eastern Railway. They took a dim view of the Pulham mast which was 120 feet high and had no elevator.

I have a very vivid memory of a flight on 17th June, when *R-36* carried 40 Members of Parliament for a flight round the coast of England to the Pulham mast from the Cardington mast. A good pick up of the mooring wires was made and the ship hauled down to the mast. The gangway was run out from the ship to my platform on the top of the mast and the MPs commenced to disembark. I realized that they had to climb down 120 feet of iron ladders inside the mast structure, but the first few took it in good part and, assisted by a petty officer below me, embarked on the descent. All seemed well until an MP with a very large stomach arrived at the head of the ladder; I eyed my round hole in the top platform. Its narrow circumference did not deter my slim body, but would it take his?

I warned my Petty Officer below me and with some trepidation explained my problem to the owner of the tummy. To my relief he burst out laughing and agreed to 'have a go'. The first 'go' merely jammed him in the hole, so assisted from below and above we hauled him up again. Then he removed his jacket and put the contents of his waistcoat pockets into the pockets of his jacket. This eased the situation and by my levering bits of tummy through the hole with my fingers and my assistant below gently pulling on the waistcoat, we got him through, with his jacket and contents following.

A few days later, on the 21st, we had real trouble. *R-36* came in for what at first appeared a normal landing; there was practically no wind at the time and after a coupling of the two wires was made, the ship had too much speed and over-rode the mast. The mooring wire then fouled the winch, the jerk releasing the two forward emergency ballast bags causing the bow to rise quickly. The ship was then brought up by a second jerk on the full length of the mooring cable, when the bow collapsed, the break taking place in the longitudinal girders aft of frame one and allowing the tubular structure on the nose to turn over and hang vertically.

R33 moored to the Pulham mast, 1921.

R33 leaving Pulham in 1926 carrying two single seater Gamecock fighters.

This second jerk was fairly severe, but as Scott pointed out in his report, 'R-33 had sustained just as severe jerks without damage and this raises the question as to the relative strength of the bows of the two ships'.

Following the accident the ship was brought slowly to the ground, gas being valved to assist the operation. A small landing party had now arrived and manned the guys. It was decided that it would not be practical to try to fly the ship to Howden, and that the only alternative was to delete Zeppelin L-64 and house R-36 in her place. This partial genocide was duly commenced. By two o'clock the following morning the landing party had been increased to 170 men and as a light wind had sprung up, the ship was walked round to the opposite end of the shed and taken under the lee of the wind screen.

At about four o'clock sufficient room was made to get R-36 about 300 feet into the shed and secured to anchor rings. Half an hour later the starboard after guy pulled out of the ship, a weak point which had been repeatedly reported, and the ship was blown onto the door and sustained damage to her port side amidship. Soon the port side forward guy pulled out, causing further damage.

The ship was got under control by manning auxiliary guys and was secured and slung by about seven o'clock in the morning.

In his report Scott took the opportunity to point out the difficulty of operating with the winch in use at that time.

R-33 was then recommissioned to carry on with the experimental work, repairs on R-36 being delayed until 1925, when it was proposed to recommission her while R-33 was having her bow rebuilt; this was never actually carried out and R-36 was deleted in 1926.

R-37 had been begun in December 1917 by Short Brothers at Cardington after Vickers had to give up the ship because of shed difficulties; in 1921 work was stopped and this ship, which was well advanced, was demolished. In late 1917 when Vickers could not carry on with R-37 they obtained permission to build a ship that *would* fit in their existing shed at Barrow, and the Barnes

Wallis *R-80* was born, a small edition of the *R-33* class and the size of the *R-23* class. *R-80* was probably the most beautiful of all the British war-time rigids, with a fully streamlined body, and had a gross lift almost two tons better than had been estimated. *R-80* first flew on 19th July 1920; her last flight was on 20th September 1921 after only 75 hours of flying, principally in training the American crew for *R-38*. *R-80* was dismantled and used for strength tests in 1925; Vickers proposed building *R-81*, but the contract was not signed.

In June 1918 the Naval Staff drew up a design for an airship suitable for use at the end of 1919. After many conferences it was considered that the Admiralty 'Design A' was the only one that could meet the requirements.

In September, 1918 an order for the first of this type was placed with Short Brothers at Cardington, Bedfordshire, to be numbered *R-38*. The order was cancelled the following January, but re-instated in February. Very soon envious eyes were cast on Cardington and the Government took it over, transactions not being completed until April 1920. By then *R-37* was well advanced and *R-38* expected by the following summer.

In the meantime the Air Ministry had officially taken over Cardington and all airships, the directive being dated 22nd October, 1919. By September the Admiralty had decided on completing *R-38* rather than to proceed with the older types, particularly as an offer to buy her had been received from the United States Navy, which offer was accepted, and the United States number *ZR-2* designated, on approval by the Cabinet.

The Americans were building *ZR-1*, the *Shenandoah*, while *ZR-3*, to be called *Los Angeles*, was the official number and name given to the Zeppelin *LZ-126* being built by the Germans for the USA.

The United States Navy crew for *R-38* was able to use *R-32*, the wooden Schutte-Lanz type airship, for training, and later *R-80*, the small Vickers ship.

R-38, USA *LZ-2* to be, had many novel innovations and apparently had not been adequately stressed, through an unfortunate chain of events. She was badly behind in building and pressure was being exercised from several quarters to speed up delivery. Tests of 150 hours had been planned, but 50 hours were suggested as being adequate. This was contested by our chief, Air Commodore Maitland, who had flown with Scott in *R-34* on her double crossing of the Atlantic, and also by Scott himself, Thomas – the Captain of *R-33* – and by Pritchard – the officer in charge of flying operations.

The pleas for longer trials were rejected and *R-38* took the air in June 1921, building having commenced in October 1919. The Germans had been building Zeppelins in ten or twelve weeks!

The first flight was of seven hours and faults were found at once, the balanced rudders were unsatisfactory and the control wires slackened up at moderate speeds. The second flight was on the 28th and 29th June and at an increased speed, control was still more difficult and modifications were carried out on the control surfaces, where also constructional weakness was found. The petrol system also had to be altered. The third flight was on July 17th and 18th from Cardington to Howden and over the North Sea, when *R-38* was found to hunt badly at 50 knots. Further modifications were carried out at Howden and damaged girders had to be replaced or strengthened.

Commander L.A.H. Maxfield, the United States Navy Officer who was to command *R-38*, was informed about this time that the Pulham mast would be at his disposal when modifications were completed after the 17th. At the same time efforts were being made to lighten the ship as much as possible for the trans-Atlantic flight.

On 23rd August, 1921, *R-38* left Howden on her fourth and last flight. Various tests were undertaken, particularly full speed runs with the rudders in different positions, and a mooring at the Pulham mast was arranged. Dusk fell and it was decided to stay out over the North Sea for the night, as there were very foggy conditions and *R-38* could not locate the Pulham Mooring Mast.

I had been waiting for news on the top of the Pulham mast for most of the day, but came down at night, returning to my post at

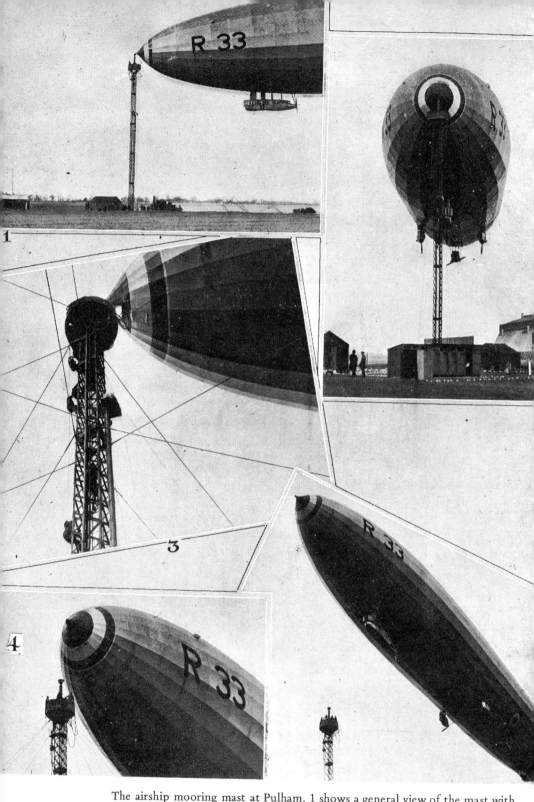

The airship mooring mast at Pulham. 1 shows a general view of the mast with R33 moored to it. 2 is a front view of the airship. 3 shows the crew climbing towards the platform, and the hydrogen supply pipe at the side of the mast can be seen. 4 shows the airship just free from the mast, and in 5 the airship rises well clear.

dawn the following morning.

R-38 was then completing her trials, including a full speed run during which she touched 62 knots. A quarter of an hour later rudder movements were carried out at about 54 knots, at a height of 2,500 feet. It was afterwards pointed out that the Zeppelin people carried out trials at at least 7,000 feet and that their rudder controls were deliberately kept heavy to prevent coxswains making violent movements.

R-38 was then over Hull and there were many witnesses to her subsequent movements. It appeared that a number of rapid changes of direction were ordered, probably involving the rudder travelling the complete arc of its possible range, which of course put enormous strain on the 700-foot airship. The ship also appeared to be diving or climbing at the same time.

In the event the ship broke her back, between frames 9 and 10 and fell into the River Humber in view of the wharves of Hull. It is presumed that petrol and the fracture of electrical mains in the forward portion of the ship caused a fire that burnt out that part of the airship. The rear part did not burn but floated down into the river. I remember that a rigger, who was in the stern lookout post, was picked up by a row boat without even getting his feet wet. Four out of the five survivors were in this part of the ship and were rescued uninjured. Most of the crew were killed. Wann, the Captain, was badly injured but saved, together with one of the National Physical Laboratory men and three of the crew.

Some time during the day of 24th August I received a message in my nest 120 feet up at the top of the mooring mast head at Pulham to come down as Major Scott wished to see me. I descended and found him waiting with Lord Ventry, both sad-eyed. Scott gave me the news, then one each side of me we walked in sorrow to the Mess. For this, the last Admiralty design, it was the end.

The Court of Enquiry found that the structure had failed, and noted that the design should have been examined by a competent committee before building was begun owing to the many novel features incorporated. Robin Higham mentions this in his book

The British Rigid Airship 1908-1931* and gives a report of a later
lecture, delivered in 1926, by Doctor Barnes Wallis

In 1913 [Barnes Wallis noted] J.E. Temple had discovered
that airships were liable to aerodynamic forces caused by the
peculiar distributions of pressures in curvilinear flight, which
was for them the norm. In other words, airships never fly
either perfectly straight or perfectly level, but in fact oscillate
about a theoretical flight path so that their actual flight path
is curvilinear. As sheer forces and bending moments increased
rapidly with size and speed, special care had to be taken with
larger ships. But this the designers of *R-38* neglected to do.
Moreover, very fine ships (*R-38*'s length to diameter ratio was
8.3:1) might, noted Wallis, be easier to build, but were not as
safe as tubbier shapes' (Quoted from Lloyd's Register Staff
Association Transactions VI February, 1926).

We that were left at Pulham were stunned at our position; but
soon got down to what had to be done. Nothing more in airship
development would be carried out until 1925. My task was the
preparation of a collective report, with photographs, on the
various methods of airship mooring for Air Ministry records,
particularly the mooring masts which had been so valuable in the
recent developments.

It is not surprising that a satisfactory method of mechanical
handling and mooring airships in the open has been constantly in
the minds of airshipmen, particularly in view of the need for large
handling parties of men otherwise. Various methods were tried out
from 1907 at Farnborough, and later at Barrow, Kingsnorth,
Pulham and Cardington.

Trials were made of mooring on the surface of land and water;
of mooring in the air on one or more wires, and later to a mooring
mast which became the standard in time as considerable man-
handling was avoided. Mooring masts were erected at Pulham; and
at Cardington, Bedfordshire, where a mast fitted with a lift was

---

* Published in 1961 by G.T. Foulis & Co. Ltd., London.

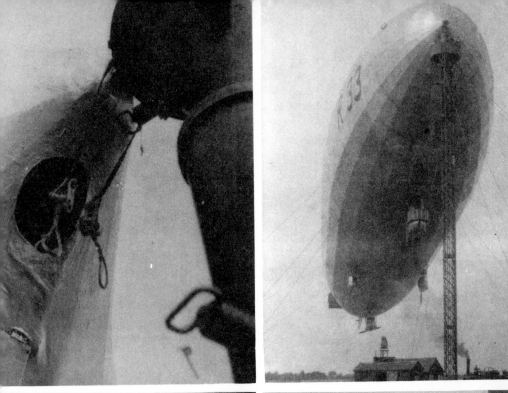

R33 on the mooring mast at Pulham. *Top left* shows a close-up view at the masthead and *right* it will be noted that access to the platform of the Pulham masthead was by ladder only. *Lower left* R33 being hauled down.

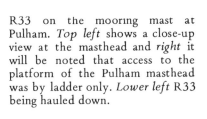

An SS attached to a
3-wire mooring

Using a quarry to
provide a protected
mooring.

An SS moored in
woodland.

built. The report by Captain Thomas on the conclusion of the trials of *R-33* at Pulham up to 21st July 1921 read:

> It was definitely proved by the foregoing experiments that the system of mooring to a mast, and leaving and landing thereto, is entirely sound; that a ship would successfully ride out all types of weather; that she could leave the mast in any weather that she could fly in; and (notably the hauling-in and yaw-guy winches) she would be able to land in winds of over 30 m.p.h. The ship did not show excessive deterioration excepting the gas bags which is probably caused by the adhesive used between the skins and the fabric. Ordinary routine work can be carried out on the ship at the mast and work such as changing an engine or a gas bag performed.

When landing a rigid to a mast, it was usually found necessary to attach yaw-wires and their winches to the fore handling guys of the airship to steady the intake of the hauling wire. The Americans evolved stub-masts and mechanical handling for their rigids, which enabled the ships either to remain in the open or to be taken into their sheds by the equipment. Towing trials of rigid *R-26* by a tank at Pulham showed some promise.

Mooring of the small non-rigids was carried out on the ground in quarries or bays cut into woods away from their bases which greatly assisted the value of their operations.

Scott, and our designer of that time, Lieutenant Colonel V.C. Richmond offered to refurbish *R-36* and fly her to the United States as some recompense for the loss of *R-38*, but this was refused both by the Air Ministry and the United States Navy.

At the end of 1921 British aviation was in a bad way. The airlines were struggling for survival, and airships were dead or moribund.

I had had a letter in May from Clayton-Kennedy asking me if I would consider carrying out an aerial survey by airship of the St. Augustine limits in Canada, the material being supplied by the Air Ministry or the Air Board of Canada, but my earlier experience of the organization in Newfoundland was not encouraging and I declined.

Chapter 14

Later Highlights to R - 102

In April 1922 I left Pulham once more as the personnel was dispersed on the cessation of airship activity after the loss of *R-38*. There was great sadness in our little company.

During the following month my financial state was improved by a cheque from the Admiralty covering my final share of the Naval Prize Fund, which was very acceptable. The Ministry of Pensions had offered me commercial training either as a school teacher or a course in mercantile law and accountancy. I did not fancy school teaching, but I recognized that a training in law and accountancy could be of considerable value to me in the future and this I accepted, starting at the Polytechnic in May. I found a fairly tough task ahead of me as instruction had commenced some months before, but there were excellent text books and I worked hard and soon caught up. At the end of the year I obtained good passes in the London Chamber of Commerce and Institute of Bookkeepers Examinations and included a Pelman Institute Certificate for good measure.

In January 1923 I was in touch with Sidney Cotton with whom I was associated in Newfoundland in 1920: he had been concerned with aeroplanes and I with airships. Cotton asked me to join him again in Newfoundland where he had several projects in hand and to take over his Companies as Secretary and General Manager as he was often away. A contract was signed with his solicitors in London on the 2nd February and I sailed from Liverpool a few days later on the SS *Digby* for St. John's, Newfoundland.

A letter dated 6th April, 1923, forwarded to me from the Air Ministry did not reach me for some weeks. The letter was the offer of a short service commission as an accountant in the Royal Air

Force, but I had to refuse it as I was under contract.

The work in Newfoundland was of an extremely diversified character which could fill another book but airships were not involved, so I will be brief.

Cotton had endeavoured to carry on with the aircraft scouting for the sealing industry and had completed the hangar at Botwood in the face of enormous difficulty, the ground being frozen solid to a depth of eighteen inches. He had got an aeroplane out to the icefield, after the sealing fleet had sailed, and was able to give some assistance, but the conditions were impossible.

The Aerial Survey Company was later formed not only to undertake aerial surveys, but to carry the mails, supply an emergency medical service and provide transport to and from a gold strike in Labrador.

Alan Butler, who became a director of the de Havilland Aircraft Company at this time and later the Chairman, became interested in our affairs; the Hawke's Bay Trading Company and the Labrador Gold Deposits Limited, was formed, with several subsidiary interests. Sydney Bennett, the son of the Colonial Secretary of Newfoundland was also a Director.

On my return to England some years later Alan Butler sent me to the headquarters of the de Havilland Aircraft Company at Edgware in Middlesex.

While in Newfoundland in 1925 I heard whispers of a resuscitation of airship activities and I wrote to Commander Sir Dennis Burney, MP, in London. He was the inventor of the paravane and originator of the airship scheme for Imperial Communications with India and Australia. I asked him for news of any moves and begged that I might not be forgotten. I had a reply in May from Major P.L. Teed whom I knew and who had been with Vickers. He wrote on behalf of the Airship Guarantee Company Limited and told me that this Company had a contract with the British Government to design and construct an airship of 5,000,000 cubic feet — but that it would not be delivered until September 1927; he promised to keep me in touch. Then came the news of the two airships, *R-100* to be built at Howden near Hull in

Yorkshire by the Vickers organization and *R-101* of the same size to be built by the Government at Cardington, Bedfordshire.

I was again in correspondence with Teed who was now at Howden where at the beginning they had a dreadful struggle to resuscitate the hydrogen plant on the old airship station. P.L. Teed wrote an article for the June 1930 issue of *Aircraft Engineering* which gives a considerable amount of detail of this for the technical reader. Teed suggested in his letters that I should apply to take charge of the Canadian Airship Mooring Mast to be built at Saint Hubert, Montreal, in view of my mooring mast experience in England. This I did at once, writing to the Royal Airship Works, as Cardington was now called, and also writing to Scott asking for his endorsement. I had a reply in April that I should apply direct to the Canadian Government, the appointment coming under its jurisdiction. I was also told that my name was recorded in connection with any future airship activities. I heard later that I had been earmarked for the projected *R-102*.

I also wrote to my old flying partner, George Meager, who had been appointed to *R-100*. He replied that he would think that I had a very good chance of getting the Canadian Mooring Mast job, but added: 'Don't panic as the ship won't be in Montreal until the summer of 1929 at the earliest'. He added, somewhat pessimistically, that in view of the experimental nature of the project, if I had a good job I should consider hanging on to it. A later letter from him gave an estimated date of February or March of 1929 for the first flight of *R-100* and June for *R-101*. These estimates were confirmed in a letter from P.L. Teed, who in a later letter told me that a recommendation for my appointment had been passed to the Royal Canadian Air Force.

I had of course made a formal application in May to Ottawa and had a reply from the Controller of the Department of Defence of a favourable nature. I decided that I should visit Ottawa. I had not been well and felt that a change would be beneficial, so took leave and travelled in the R.N.S. *Rosalind* of the Red Cross Line from St John's up the St Lawrence River to Montreal, then by train to Ottawa. I was very well received by the authorities and had interviews with the Canadian Air Minister. As it was obvious that no on the spot decision was going to be available I travelled on to New York, the latter being most interesting for a visit, but no more. I had booked a berth on the RNS *Newfoundland* for St John's but was delayed in getting to the wharf and she left without me; so I went by train via Boston, the coast of Maine and St John, New Brunswick. I caught the steamer at Halifax, Nova Scotia, back to St John's.

A letter arrived from Ottawa in September in reply to my enquiry saying that no decision had yet been reached regarding the Canadian Mooring Mast. I felt that this uncertainty could go on indefinitely and as the thought of another winter in Newfoundland was intolerable I decided to return to England. I settled my affairs, selling my business interests and house in St John's, Newfoundland. When I was ready to leave I found that a Norwegian steamer in which we were concerned was about to leave for the Mediterranean with a cargo of dried cod, so I signed on as Supercargo and had a leisurely crossing of the Atlantic.

Our first call was at Seville in the south of Spain, a gay city on the Guadalquivir River, which coincided with a long fiesta, so we had to tie up to a wharf and wait through a series of jollifications in which we joined; and bull fights, in which we did not join, excepting to cheer the bull on one occasion, which was not appreciated. We finally completed unloading our quota and went on to Gibraltar where I unloaded myself on the 16th October, 1928. I had a weeks rest while waiting for the White Star liner *Orama* homeward bound from Australia, calling in at Plymouth, which latter looked like heaven to me.

A letter had just arrived in London from Ottawa saying that it had been decided to appoint a Canadian Naval Officer to take charge of the Montreal Mooring Mast and that he, with four naval ratings had left for England for a course of instruction. I had felt that this was a possibility so was not too greatly shocked.

In the meantime the building struggle had been going on with *R-100* at Howden, and *R-101* at Cardington. George Meager had given me some indication of the difficulties, delays and uncertainties. The first flights appeared to be years away. I had little hope of getting on the crew of either ship, and R-102 was only in the design stage.

Nevil Shute in his book *Slide Rule* gives striking details of the hazards, particularly, I think, in his account of testing the Rolls Royce Condor engines of *R-100* in the tight shed at Howden with no space at all to spare.*

On 6th November 1929, George Meager had tested a small private enterprise non-rigid for her Certificate of Airworthiness which ship later carried out work flown by Beckford-Ball, a World War One airship pilot. The airship, called *AD-1* was similar to an early SS of 60,000 cubic feet and had a car similar to a BE 2c. The engine was an ABC Hornet of 75 horsepower.

R-100 made her first flight on 16th December 1929 and after trials in the vicinity of Howden flew to Cardington to join *R-101*. There was great disappointment here, apparently due to the lack of experience of the landing officer. Three circuits had to be made before a connection with the ship's mooring wire was made — which made me feel sick when I heard about it. *R-100* flew again next day taking advantage of the quiet weather conditions. They were anxious to do speed trials, as Cardington would not believe that *R-100* was ten miles an hour faster than *R-101* which had first flown on the 14th October, two months previously. *R-100* landed in a thick mist that would have baffled an aeroplane. She was taken into the shed on landing and housed beside *R-101* while teething troubles were gone into, which were cured by the middle of January 1930. She flew again on the 18th when full speed trials were possible; she achieved a speed of eighty-one miles per hour. Another flight was made on the 22nd to investigate deformations of the outer cover at speed.

The final acceptance trial was on 27th January, with a flight of fifty-four hours, the ship landing on the 29th having behaved very well indeed in very bad weather and was handed over to the Air Ministry.

* Published by William Heinemann, London 1954.

R101 on the Cardington mast, which was provided with a lift.

A promenade deck of R101.
The lounge of R101

R-100 did not fly again until May when some girder trouble was detected in the tail, which was modified. In accordance with the contract, preparation was made for a flight to Canada, with a further flight in July, of twenty-four hours, her seventh journey.

On 29th July, 1930, *R-100* slipped the mast at Cardington in the early morning heading across the Atlantic for Montreal. She moored at the mast there at dawn 78 hours out from Cardington, staying in Montreal for twelve days, during which a local flight was made with Canadian passengers, lasting twenty-four hours. This was in 1930: I need not have hurried in 1928.†

On 13th August the ship left the mast at Montreal at ten in the morning and landed at the Cardington mast on the 16th, 57½ hours later. This was the last flight of *R-100*. A.H. Wann the surviving Captain from *R-38* was a passenger on her Atlantic flight.

There was great rivalry between the constructors of the *R-100* and *R-101* and as it became evident that *R-100* was the better ship, the pressure to put in a major flight with *R-101* became more evident.

It was rumoured that *R-101* had difficulty in keeping aloft on her return to Cardington after a visit to the Hendon Air Show; she first flew on the 14th October, 1929, and it soon became obvious that she could not carry out her test flight to India as her disposable lift was insufficient; quite early on excessive gas leaks had developed. It was decided to part her in the middle and fit an additional bay to allow one more gasbag. This was duly done, and other alterations were made, such as fitting two of her engines with reversible gears.

After the return of *R-100* from Canada in August 1930, every effort was made to put *R-101* into a condition to be able to carry out her India flight. The task was fantastic. After the new bay and reversing engines were fitted, all the controls had to be re-positioned; the leaking valves, chafing gas bags, and faulty outer cover had to be attended to. The date given by Lord Thomson of Cardington, the Labour Government Secretary of State for Air,

† See 'My Airship Flights' by Captain George Meager. William Kimber 1970.

was 4th October and he was to travel in the ship to India.

With great efforts the *R-101* was got out of the shed at Cardington and on to the mast on 2nd October; she made a flight of sixteen hours during the next two days but engine trouble prevented a full power test. The last flight of *R-101* commenced at six-thirty in the evening of Saturday 4th October, 1930. In addition to the crew there were six passengers, including Lord Thomson, and six officials from the Royal Airship Works.

The weather report was not good at the time, with a later report indicating a deterioration. Scott, who was in charge, must have been in grave difficulty. He was flying an airship that had never been in the air in really bad weather and had not carried out full speed tests, but then he was presumably under the orders of the Secretary of State for Air.

The airship crossed the English Channel slowly in a gusty head-wind. The weather forecasting was not so reliable as today, but foretold stronger winds to come. One engine had broken down and was under repair for two hours. At two in the early morning of the fifth, the watch was changed, indicating that no trouble was expected, but ten minutes later the airship was a burning wreck on the ground near Beauvais. She had landed quite lightly and at a low speed, but the collapse of possibly the centre structure had probably caused electrical sparks from broken cables to ignite leaking gas and petrol.

There wee fifty-four persons on board and only six survived, four being engineers in the power cars. All the officers and passengers were killed. The true cause of the tragedy was never established, but from the evidence, I think the most likely was that a large portion of the outer cover failed in the bow, which was known to be faulty, followed by the emptying of the forward gas bag. This caused the bow to drop and the ship to dive, when she was too low to recover. There is no doubt that she was a bad ship, as had been *R-38* before her.

The French and the British jointly built a granite memorial on the site at Beauvais, which I visited later.

On 23rd October the Committee of Preliminary Investigation

Above: R101 on the Cardington mast.
Below: R100 on the landing ground and R101 on the mooring mast at Cardington in October 1930.

handed in it's report, but drew no conclusions excepting that *R-101* had come into contact with the ground and had not broken in the air. There were numerous opinions as to the cause. The loss of the airship was a grievous blow, not only to the comparatively few airship men remaining, but to the general public, who had been told for years of the wonders of British rigid airships and their capabilities, and had in fact seen them flying overhead. After the initial shock was over there was a hope that we would live it down as we had after the loss of *R-38*. We still had *R-100* with the successful crossing to Canada and back behind her; and the *Graf Zeppelin* was voyaging like a liner. The declared cost of *R-100* was given as £411,113 and the *R-101* as £717,165.

There has been no rigid airship work in this country since, excepting the visits of the *Graf Zeppelin*. In March 1930 the Royal Airship Works at Cardington had produced designs for an 8,300,000 cubic feet airship to be called *R-102*, but no further action was taken.

Chapter 15

Airship History brought up-to-date

I had now joined the de Havilland Aircraft Company Limited at Stag Lane, Edgware, my accountancy training and experience serving in good stead — as it has done often in my life. I felt that R-102 was now probably further away than ever.

One day I was sitting in my office talking to a metal merchant about the disposal of scrap material. He told me this story, without knowing mine. 'Some time ago', he said, 'I was asked to go to France to make an offer for the remains of the airship R-101. It was a difficult task scrambling amongst girders and sliding about in what had been the keel on human fat . . .'. At this point I stopped him, saying: 'You are speaking of my friends!'

The disaster to R-101 caused the cessation of all airship work in England. The design staff of R-100 at Howden were dispersed at the end of 1930 and the design work on R-102, was discontinued.

In the meantime R-100 remained at the Royal Airship Works at Cardington and she needed a new outer cover. Robin Higham states in *The British Rigid Airship* that counting up the initials on a memorandum initiated on 26th June, 1929 about the new outer cover showed that it had passed through 54 hands before it was closed in April 1931; while the minute on the sale of R-38 was handled by 208 people! In contrast Imperial Airways employed seven men to run a world wide airline.

R-100 was offered to foreign governments without result. Nothing was announced as to her fate for some time, when it became known that she had been torn apart and sold for scrap, her last flight being a successful double crossing of the Atlantic. Thus was treated the most successful and promising of the British rigid airships. The Captain of R-100, R.S. Booth, died in September

Akron in 1931.

Macon in 1933.

1969 just before the emergence of a book by his chief officer, George Meager, describing his flights. Cardington remains a Royal Air Force Station.

A curious article appeared in the *Sunday Dispatch* of 19th March, 1933, written by Harry Price, Director of the National Laboratory of Psychical Research, giving a detailed report on a spiritualist seance held just previously in which Captain H.C. Irwin, who was the Captain of *R-101* when she was lost, was stated to have described details of the flight, which were remarkably credible.*

I have made no attempt to record the activities of First World War Zeppelins, as there are many books already available about them. Some attention must be paid to airships activities, however, in other parts of the world after the 1914-1918 war.

In 1919 an American non-rigid the *C-5* of 180,000 cubic feet flew from Montauk, Long Island, to St. John's, Newfoundland, in just over 26 hours, averaging fifty miles per hour. It was intended to attempt an Atlantic crossing, but while the two pilots were resting and the ship was being refuelled, a storm arose and tore her away from her moorings, with no one on board, and she disappeared out to sea. This C Class airship was one of ten used by the USA during the War. Of three main types some 32 had been in operation, built either by Goodyear, or by Goodrich. Of the American-built rigids, *ZR-1* — the *Shenandoah* — of 2,000,000 cubic feet, flew from 1923 to 1925; the *Akron* from 1931 to 1933 and the *Macon* from 1933 to 1935. Both of the latter were of 6,500,000 cubic feet. They were numbered *ZR-4* and *ZR-5* respectively. *ZR-2* was the number allotted to *R-38* bought from the British, while *ZR-3* was the Zeppelin-built *LZ-126* flown to the United States in 1924 by Dr. Hugo Eckener and named the *Los Angeles*. This was the star ship of the American rigids, flying continuously for nine years, retained on the ground for another seven years, and dismantled only in 1939.

This remarkable airship, was comparable with the famous *Graf*

* See also *The Millionth Chances* by James Leasor. Hamish Hamilton 1967.

Zeppelin herself. The *Los Angeles* of 2,500,000 cubic feet and 656 feet in length was completed by the Germans at Friedrichshafen in August 1924 and then flown to Lakehurst in the United States.

Unlike most airships she had comfortable quarters for passengers and crew, with a modern kitchen that could produce regular meals. For many years she carried important persons to events all over the United States and never suffered any major damage.

Some 331 flights, totalling 4,320 flying hours, and 2,000 hours riding at the mooring mast, can be claimed. She landed on the deck of the USA aircraft carrier *Saratoga* at sea on a very gusty day; and on another occasion picked up an aeroplane on a trapeze, the pilot going on board the airship.

On 30th June, 1932, during the American financial depression, *Los Angeles* was grounded for reasons of economy and never flew again. Like the *Graf Zeppelin* she died in her bed.

The *Akron ZRS-4* first flew on 23rd September 1931, and the *Macon ZRS-5* on 21st April 1933; both these ships were of 6,500,000 cubic feet, and both were lost in accidents.

The United States became interested in semi-rigids in 1921 and bought the *Roma* from Italy, which was built and delivered by air by Colonel Umberto Nobile, whom we had met in Italy in 1918. He was concerned in the building of our *SR-1* flown to England in that year by George Meager and myself. The *Roma* landed heavily next year owing to the breaking of a control, but not sufficiently to injure any of the crew. She unfortunately fouled some high tension cables at the same time and was destroyed.

Nobile was also concerned with two other international semi-rigid flights, the *Norge* in 1926 with which a successful flight was made over the North Pole, when American, Italian and Norwegian flags were planted there. Two years later the *Italia*, a larger Italian semi-rigid, again flown by Nobile, failed to make a North Pole crossing and some of the crew were rescued with difficulty.

The polar explorer, Roald Amundsen, whom I had met previously in Newfoundland and had tried unsuccessfully to persuade into taking me on an Arctic expedition, was lost in an aeroplane while searching for Nobile. He was the only man in the world, at that time, to have seen both Poles.

In 1928, following the Zeppelin *LZ-126*, the *Los Angeles*, came *LZ-127* the *Graf Zeppelin*, the greatest airship of all time, with Dr. Hugo Eckener as pilot. She did a circuit of the world the following year, in 21 days and during her 650 flights, including 144 crossings of the Atlantic, and a million miles, carried more than 18,000 passengers without a fatality.

In August of 1931 we landed the *Graf Zeppelin* at London Air Park at Hanworth, to the west of London. We had no mooring mast, but only a vast handling party to do the work. The ship made a twenty-four hour flight round the British Isles carrying prominent persons in aeronautics and members of the press. A further visit by the *Graf Zeppelin* was made to Hanworth on 3rd July the following year when George Meager was in charge of the landing party. S.E. Taylor was on the starboard side of the ship and I took the port side — three Kingsnorth-trained airship pilots together again!

In 1924 while I was in Hawke's Bay in the extreme north of Newfoundland where my only transport in the winter was my team of dogs, about the time we were endeavouring to run an airline to the Labrador gold strike at Stag Bay, I was appointed a Special Correspondent of the *Chicago Tribune* to report 'The First World Flight'. My duties included long telegrams to Chicago, covering every detail of the movements of the two aeroplane-cum-seaplanes which reached us out of an original fleet of four. The planes were manufactured in California by the Douglas Aircraft Corporation, had 450 horsepower Liberty engines and weighed about 4 tons each. They were named *Seattle, Boston, New Orleans* and *Chicago*, and started from Seattle on 6th April, travelling west round the northern hemisphere via Alaska, Japan, Hongkong, Burma, India, Aleppo, Baghdad, Constantinople, Bucharest, Vienna, Paris, London, the Orkneys, Iceland, Greenland, Newfoundland, Labrador — where only two were now still flying, the *Chicago* and the *New Orleans*. The flight was then completed via

Above left: Graf Zeppelin at Hanworth in 1932.
Above right: Hugo Eckener appearing at a window of *Graf Zeppelin.*
Below: Graf Zeppelin on the landing ground at Cardington 28th April 1930, with R100 on the mooring mast.

Nova Scotia, Boston, New York, Washington, Chicago, Los Angeles and San Francisco. It had taken 175 days and several engine replacements and repairs, generally carried out en route by the United States Navy.

Later, in May 1927, I went out to the Cabot Tower on the headland at St. John's with a team of observers. Dusk was falling on a quiet evening as we looked out over the sea and at last appeared what we had come for; a tiny monoplane flown by a pilot named Charles Lindbergh, made at St. Louis by the Ryan Company and fitted with a 225 h.p. Wright Whirlwind engine.

The little aeroplane made a circuit round us then turned to the east over the Atlantic and was soon lost to sight in the gathering darkness. It had flown from New York, and after a flight of 33½ hours landed in Paris! It was the first solo flight across the Atlantic and that was bravery indeed! It was certainly a more hazardous flight than a trip to the moon today.

Stimulated by the activities of the *Graf Zeppelin*, the nineteen-thirties seemed a time of enhanced interest in airships for several countries abroad. Russia built some non-rigids, and constructed hangars at Leningrad and Moscow. Spain considered erecting a mooring mast at Seville for use on the South American Service, carried out by the *Graf Zeppelin*. France built a semi-rigid, the *E9*, which made its first flight on 10th January, 1933, from Orly.

The *Graf Zeppelin* continued to make airship history with regular fortnightly flights across the South Atlantic during the summer of 1933, 1934 and 1935. The pilot was usually Hugo Eckener, probably the greatest of all airship captains. He died in 1954. •

LZ-128 the next in the Zeppelin series was never constructed, but *LZ-129* of 7,000,000 cubic feet, the largest airship built so far, was launched in 1936, and became the commercial airship *Hindenburg*. This airship carried out ten flights in considerable comfort between Germany and the United States before she was destroyed when mooring at Lakehurst in May 1937. It should be noted that the 13 passengers lost on this occasion, possibly by sabotage, were the only fatalities experienced in all commercial airship flights.

The Germans completed *LZ-130*, named *Graf Zeppelin II* in September 1938 and were allotted a helium ration by the United States, then the only source of supply, but this was refused later as war clouds appeared. The two *Graf Zeppelins* remained in their hangars during the latter part of 1939 but were dismantled in 1940.

Between the two wars the United States retained some of their non-rigid airships, eight being in commission in the United States Naval Airship Service, based on Lakehurst, at the beginning of World War II. Extensive patrols were carried out during the Second World War, something like 89,000 surface ships being escorted without loss. They had a squadron of non-rigids in the Meditterranean, some even had flown the South Atlantic on delivery flights. About 150 non-rigids at 15 stations mostly of the K and M Classes being in use — some coastal work was continued with them until 1961.

I spent most of the period of World War Two with the de Havilland Aircraft Company at Stag Lane, Edgware, as Office Manager and Assistant to the Financial Director. I had made several visits to the Continent on contractual matters, and took a prominent part in the move of the headquarters of the company to Hatfield, and previously had attended to the ground non-flying arrangements of the King's Cup Air Race for some years.

At Stag Lane we were left responsible for the production of Gipsy engines, particularly for the Tiger Moth trainer, also for variable-pitch airscrews for the Royal Air Force. At first we were the only source of supply of this type of airscrew, other than imports, until later we built a shadow factory at Lostock, near Bolton in Lancashire. Later also we had to attend to the repair of Merlin engines from Spitfire and Hurricane aeroplanes, and sometimes to pick up the pieces of fighters and bombers which had crashed in the neighbourhood. For the repair of Rolls-Royce Merlins I had the task of commandeering suitable factories in the vicinity, and to attend to the factory defence of our several units, for which purpose I was once more put into uniform: this time an

Top: the *Hindenburg* the last of the commercial Zeppelin's in 1937. *Bottom* The last Zeppelin. *Graf Zeppelin* II on her maiden flight September 14th 1938.

Army one, as a Major in the Middlesex Regiment which gave me my third commission. I had to attend to my office work in my spare time! Some years later I received a Defence Medal by post in recognition of my services in the Second World War.

Stag Lane was under aerial bombardment frequently, more particularly at night. I spent many nights on the tower of the factory over my office with the Observer Corps men, having a bed to retire to below if circumstances permitted. At times bombs, both high-explosive and incendiary, almost seemed to rain down around us.

I can still see, in my mind's eye, a peak of searchlight beams following the movements of an enemy aeroplane, perhaps coming straight towards us. A bell-push on a long lead in one's hand connected with alarm bells in the workshops. Would the raider turn off the track? It was being heavily fired on by anti-aircraft guns: the tracers travelling up like jewelled necklaces. If it did not turn away, at what point should the bells be rung, when the workers would leave their machine and benches and shelter in the trenches beside them? How far could men's lives be risked to get the utmost production for war purposes? And the risk included the loss of skilled men. A sickening decision to have to make.

As it was, the main Stag Lane factory escaped with only some wrecked fencing, but not all it's subsidiaries. I remember one nearby raid very well. I lived in Hampstead, when I could get there, where from the high roof of my block of flats I could see parts of London in flames night after night. I had got home early one evening to get some papers to go to a meeting at Hatfield and travelled in my car to pass near Stag Lane. The air-raid sirens were also wailing early that evening and as dusk fell so did the bombs. I saw a fire in the distance to my left and decided to go a bit closer as it appeared to be in the Stag Lane area. I found that a factory of ours a street away from Stag Lane in which we were repairing Merlin engines had been hit. The light was coming from a blazing gas-main in the street outside. As I stopped by the wrecked building on a carpet of broken glass an air-raid warden ran towards me shouting for me to put out my hooded car-lights. I did so at once with apologies, and only later realized the futility of it in an area as light as day with the gas-main burning brightly.

When I was able to travel home at nights and a raid started, which was quite usual, I would feel very small and alone with practically no other traffic. I would switch off my car lights the streets being illuminated by the reflection of searchlight beams, gun flashes and bursting bombs. I had some small comfort in my steel helmet and the steel top fitted to my car to ward off the shell splinters falling around.

Soon after getting home one night incendiary bombs fell in showers beside my flat, setting fire to Augustus John's studio below my bedroom window, but we were able to save most of his pictures. A nunnery was hit on the other side of the flats on another night, destroying it and leaving the shattered trees in front littered with torn clothing. The block of flats further down the road was presented with a parachute bomb caught by the rigging in the chimneys and swinging gently to and fro in the quadrangle. On another occasion I picked up a man in the street who had been blown through the door of his house. He looked like a snow-man covered in plaster from the ceiling.

One of the earliest raids on Stag Lane destroyed a house just beyond the boundary. One survivor sent us continual messages from hospital asking if we had yet found her false teeth.

Very vivid memories arise as I write. The great hall of Harrow School clearly visible set alight by incendiaries, probably meant for us. Apparently complete houses leaping into the air and disintegrating. The great flashes of light and shattering explosions.

Towards the end of the war I was sent into the country to rest as I was used up — as indeed had happened to me at the end of the First World War. One of my particular recollections of this time was while rusticating; I was sitting watching the water in a quiet stream go by and was challenged by a country policeman to prove my identity. I laid out about a score of passes and permits with photographs of myself on the grassy bank beside me and asked him to take his pick. The impressed official decided that my documentation was ample enough!

Although I was still involved in aviation, the war for me had little to do with airships and after it I took up farming, following my maternal ancestors, and bought a farm in Yorkshire to breed beef stock. Deciding to move south in the summer of 1951, where it would be warmer and less smoky, we bought a farm in Cornwall, hiring a complete train from British Railways and moving the farm stock intact.

I was so much involved at this time that I could not assist Lord Ventry, the great supporter of airships, who in this year showed his faith by building the *Bournemouth*, a small non-rigid of 50,000 cubic feet. The envelope was made from an observation balloon and a car constructed to carry four people, fitted with a 76-horsepower engine to give a cruising speed of 30 to 35 miles per hour. This ship successfully carried out several flights. There was otherwise then very little airship activity, excepting of course Goodyears of Akron Ohio, the most persistent of airship builders, who from the *Wingfoot Express* of July 1919 to October 1969 had built 286 airships and by the time the *Europa* came to England in 1972 the total score was 300!

Chapter 16

The Present and Future of Airships

On 18th July, 1966 the BBC gave a television broadcast about airships called 'Shadow in the Clouds'. The *Radio Times* description of the programme was headed with the words appearing in the dry docked tea-clipper, *Cutty Sark* at Greenwich:

They mark our passage as a race of men
Earth will not see such ships as these again.

It was a touching and sympathetic performance showing the BBC at its best. The broadcast ended with the last of the great rigids, the Zeppelin *Hindenburg*, expiring on landing at the mooring mast at Lakehurst on that fateful day of 6th May 1937 and the recorded voice of the American broadcaster, who spoke with great emotion of the tragedy unfolding before his eyes. There is little doubt that had the *Hindenburg* been filled with helium instead of hydrogen this would not have happened and the future of airships could have been assured; nor is it certain that the tragedy was actually an accident.

As the *Radio Times* asked: 'Is it really the end of the story?' There are those of us who are looking for the phoenix to rise from the ashes; perhaps we should join with J.A. Sinclair in his final words of *'Famous Airships of the World'*: 'Airships have not passed into history; they still make it'. Douglas Botting's description in the *Radio Times* goes on to say:

Flying to New York or Rio on board the Hindenburg, the largest and the most luxurious aircraft ever flown, you could wine and dine with the elite of Europe and America, dance on a ballroom floor, take a shower, sleep in splendid private cabins and watch flying fishes from picture windows set in the side of the ship's huge hull. The transatlantic flight took only fifty or sixty hours and no one was ever sea sick — an ideal alternative, it would seem, to the slow sea voyage or the quick but uncomfortable aeroplane flight.

There is no doubt of the discomfort of aeroplane flight. Lufthansa International recently issued an illustrated booklet called 'We'll do all we can' which sums it up in pictures. The descriptions under the pictures speak for themselves, I think. There is the figure of a man in all of them looking utterly harrassed.

1. The Departure Lounge. Alias the Waiting Room.
2. The coach to the plane. 60 passengers. 25 seats.
3. The Great Seat Stampede.
4. Lack of space between the seats and how to get over it.
5. Meal time is no time for a spread.
6. Trying to get some sleep. It's a nightmare.
7. The early morning loo queue.
8. Last one off's a cissy.
9. Your first taste of the local customs.

What a contrast; and added to this a major engine failure means almost certain disaster. Only by the brute force of excellent engines is it possible to keep in the air at all.

I have flown in every type of aircraft ever since there was flight, from the earliest days to the latest jets, including gliders and helicopters. I have flown in or watched aeroplanes fly in many countries in Europe, America, Asia and Australasia; and always there is the sense of the aeroplane hanging on a thread. During fourteen years with the de Havilland Aircraft Company I had many opportunities of seeing aeroplanes in action, and out of it. One of my duties in the Second World War was to requisition factories to be used for the repair of Spitfire and Hurricane Merlin engines, so I saw some damage.

Writing of de Havillands reminds me that while getting some Gipsy engine instruction in the Technical School, I was paired up with a charming elderly lady for the dismantling of an engine. After the class was over I discovered that she was the Duchess of Bedford who, in 1937, disappeared in the English Channel while flying her Gipsy-Moth. I was also in close touch with the pioneers such as Amy Johnson and Jim Mollison. Why this outburst? I am an airship man and in the period following World War II, in spite of all the advances, nothing was attempted here in the airship field except for Lord Ventry's gallant effort in 1951 and the AD1. There was a period of absolute quiescence, except in the United States of America and Germany.

In 1963 there were at least four non-rigids in operation, two by the Goodyear Company in the United States and two used for advertising by private businesses in Germany; the *Schwab* of Harau at Stuttgart and the Trumpf Company at Mulheim. The latter were of the United States Navy L Class of 1927. *Schwab* came from America in 1956 while *Trumpf* was built in Germany to an American design, with modifications to bring it more in line with recent developments, making it a faster craft with a greater range, and also enabling it to be handled by a smaller ground crew.

Lord Ventry had a flight in the *Schwab* in 1969, and Harold Wingham, now building the *Gloster* airship, of which I will give details later, flew in this airship some years before and wrote an excellent account of it. It was originally published in *Shell Aviation News*, and he has kindly allowed me to quote from it.

'The German and American ships are all non-rigids or blimps (Harold Wingham writes), occasionally and more accurately known as pressure ships, for there is nothing flabby or balloon-like in their appearance or behaviour. The terms mean that they have no air frame to support the form of the envelope, the shape being maintained entirely by internal pressure. Impossibly low though the figures seems, only about one ounce per square inch is necessary; and this produces enough tension in the envelope to permit a man to crawl across the top, making only the slightest impression on the fabric. Expansion and contraction of the gas from changes of altitude, atmospheric pressure and temperature is compensated for by two internal air bags or ballonets, one forward and one aft. These ballonets are filled with air by means of air scoops, located behind the propellers in order to take advantage of the slipstream. Each scoop is divided down the centre, one half feeding each ballonet, so that in the event of an engine being stationary the other can still fill both.

'Pressure is controlled by large air valves, set to lift automatically at a lower pressure than the gas valve, so that should expansion occur air is blown off rather than gas. Spring loaded dampers at the entrance to the scoops act both as non-return valves and as a control over the amount of air accepted. They and the valves can also be operated manually to vary the proportion of air in each bag; gas is thereby displaced toward the bow or stern, to trim the ship.

'The season's work begins in February with repairs and rigging, for the ships are stored during the winter months. When this stage is sufficiently advanced they are inflated with hydrogen, usually towards the end of March. *Trumpf* is inflated and rigged inside her own hangar at Mulheim, while *Schwab* is inflated in an aeroplane hangar at Stuttgart, the final rigging and attachment of the car being carried out on the field. Once fully rigged she does not enter a hangar again for the rest of the season, which lasts until the end of October, the whole time being spent either in the air or riding at a mast on an open airfield. During these months each ship usually manages to fly 800-1,000 hours, which compares well with fixed wing utilization for a whole year.

'*Schwab* has begun to last two or three of her seasons with a few months in Holland, advertising a brand of cigarettes. Advertising panels along the sides of the ship are laced on and can be changed quite easily. The drill is to spend about a week each at a number of carefully chosen and well scattered airfields, and from these to cruise over the surrounding country and centres of population. On the last day at each location the ship sets off for a long cruise, of eight hours or more, which terminates at the next

The *Trumpf* in 1969.

The car of the *Schwab*.

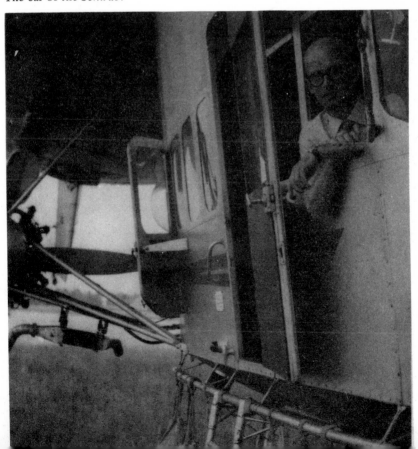

field on the itinerary. This gives the ground staff plenty of time to dismantle the small portable mast, stow it in the mobile workshop, drive to the rendezvous and have the mast re-erected before the ship's arrival. Maintenance and daily inspections are carried out with the ship riding at the mast. In changeable winds the craft weathercocks slowly from one direction to another, the ground crew solemnly tramping backwards and forwards to their work like a tango filmed in slow motion.

'I was determined to sample lighter than air travel. *Schwab* was due to move to Mulheim from Kassell within a day or two, so off I went to Mulheim and awaited the ship there. She was preceded as usual by the ground crew, who erected the portable mooring mast alongside the mobile workshop so quickly and quietly that few could have realized they had arrived. Herbert Vogtschmidt, the ship's PRO and himself an airship pilot, welcomed me at the airport just as *D-LAVO* appeared over the horizon. While we walked the two hundred and fifty yards out to the mast, calling at Air Traffic on the way, the ship had joined the circuit, made her final approach and landing, and was already riding at moorings.

'Time for a quick peer upwards at her awe-inspiring size before the captain and co-pilot, Konrad Hess and Herr Peters, returned from the control tower, but no time to suggest that it might after all be better to leave my trip until tomorrow, or to consider the proximity of all that hydrogen. "She's a bit light today and we need some ballast" they said. "You're just about the right weight: in you get".

'The speed with which the ship lifts off as soon as the throttles are opened is startling, even for people used to flying. Before I had reached my seat we were already fifty feet off the ground and climbing steeply. This type of craft is operated slightly heavier than air, and is flown off the ground and landed with a short run, power on rather like a light aeroplane; but her landing speed is no more than a gentle trot, even on a windless day, and the take off run is ten yards or less. Routine releasing of gas or ballast — especially the former — is now a thing of the past.

'I searched for my seat belt. A bit late, but never mind. "Safety belts?" queried Captain Hess. "There aren't any. The ride here is so smooth and free from bumps that they just aren't needed". He was quite right, for airsickness in airships is almost unknown: moreover, they give a feeling of confidence and relaxation that no other craft can give, on land, sea or in the air. All who have ever flown in them say the same. We were flying in very hot weather, through thermals and their bumps, yet none was felt at any time; instead, there was a slow, gentle, almost inperceptible rising and sinking of the bows, to be observed rather than felt.

'One's feeling of security is reinforced, too, by the extraordinarily high safety record enjoyed by the non-rigid airship, though this has somewhat lost impact by being confused in the public mind with the record of the large rigids. And even with these it should be remembered that the first fare paying passenger flights being in 1912, and continued (except for the war years) without a single injury until thirteen passengers were lost in the *Hindenburg* tragedy in 1937. Again, this would certainly have never happened had she been helium filled as originally intended; nor is it certain that it was an accident. But that is another story.

'At 500 feet the ship levelled out, the engines were brought back to cruise revs, and the noise level, never very high even at full throttle, fell until the cabin was quieter than the average family car. There was no aerodynamic noise and the most obvious sounds — if obvious they could be called — were a remote hum and a gentle ticking from the rocker gears.

'Take off had been at 4.30 p.m. and the next three hours we spent cruising lazily over the Ruhr. It was surprising to find how much of it was agricultural, woodland or residential, and how little seemed occupied by industry. Perhaps it was just distance and altitude lending enchantment to a summer's evening.

'Our landing was complicated by the appearance of a light aeroplane making a simultaneous approach to the runway on our right. At a height of fifty feet and with no more than 20 mph on the airspeed indicator Captain Hess pulled *Schwab* round in a turn to the left, a turn so tight that its diameter could hardly have been more than three times the ship's own length. It was interesting to see that in a turn these craft bank in the same way as a winged aircraft.

'Next day we took off at midday and flew until eight in the evening, covering the Ruhr, the Radevarme Wald and the surrounding country. During the afternoon *Trumpf*, our sister ship, climbed up toward us and kept formation for a while. Then followed what appeared to be a game of chasing over the local towns. From the ground it must have looked like a pair of porpoises playing tag. We flew around the television mast at Dortmund, with its pleasure gardens below, and then over a nearby race course. It was Sunday and a religious gathering was being held there. The roads for two miles around were thick with people, converging on the meeting

'Later, over Radevarme at about 1200 feet, Captain Hess suddenly remarked "I see Scotsmen". Far below was a drum and pipe band playing at an international sports meeting. They are in great demand in Germany for such occasions, apparently. We circled down and came to a halt just outside the arena, at a height of a couple of hundred feet; hovering there motionless, vibration-less and in complete silence the proceedings could be watched as if from a high balcony, and with binoculars and elbows braced upon the ledge of the open window, each face could be observed individually.

'We climbed away and made our way back to Mulheim by easy stages at 1,500 feet. Every three or four minutes a solitary white butterfly would drift by our windows. We called on small towns, open air meetings and small airstrips with a low, slow fly past.

'It was dusk by the time we reached our temporary base at Mulheim, recognizable by its tall radar mast and the lofty hangar built for *Trumpf*. She herself joined up with us again over the airfield, both ships now using their navigation lights. The sensation of landing in a craft of this type, especially on a calm evening, is just like coming up to moorings in a sailing cruiser, with the mainsails down and the auxiliary engine ticking over — an impression heightened by the sight of handling and mooring lines swaying from the bows.

'A few days later *Schwab* set up base at Bonn and from there we made the most interesting trip of all. It took us to Solingen, across country to the Black Forest and finally back down the Rhine, most of it at low level. Just outside Solingen we came to a halt over a garden party, so that a couple of guests on board could chat to friends below.

'Across country to the Black Forest we avoided the big towns, flying at 500 feet, sometimes less, over lonely farms and hamlets. Leaning out of the open windows every scene of the countryside came up to meet us, pine woods, hay fields and farmyards; all quite distinct and unadulterated by petrol or oil fumes. Everywhere we went people waved frantically. Children playing in the gardens ran indoors to fetch the whole family out, all waving handkerchiefs and even tablecloths. As everyone on board was clearly expected to wave in reply, it got rather tiring after a few hours. Dogs jumped and barked, cattle and horses seemed mildly curious, poultry scattered in all directions.

'Over the Black Forest we floated, with handling ropes just clearing the tree tops, up and down the hills and in and out of the valleys. A hare loped up one winding footpath ahead of us; it was almost possible to count his whiskers.

'Further on we were able to see down through the tree tops, and watch deer running along the forest paths. Over compact villages looking like toys and dozens of picnic parties, over a little gliding club operating from an open hilltop, and of course, across miles of trees. The unique feature of all airship flying is the amount of intimate detail one sees; everything stands out clear and sharp, because there is time to look, and especially because one's vision is not blurred by vibration nor the brain numbed by noise.

'As evening fell we left the higher ground and soon found ourselves cruising down the Rhine Valley towards Bonn. The air was so still that the ship was almost flying herself – a slight movement of the rudder pedals or elevator wheel now and again, very occasionally a pull at one of the toggles controlling ballonet pressure. We flew between the high banks of the river with their castles standing out in silhouette against the orange sky, over the

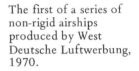

The first of a series of non-rigid airships produced by West Deutsche Luftwerbung, 1970.

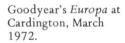

Goodyear's *Europa* at Cardington, March 1972.

Hot air airship at Compton Dando, Somerset on 29th July 1973.

pleasure steamers and the convoys of barges; finally, with the evening mist beginning to rise, to another dusk landing at the little grass airfield of Hangelar, just outside the city.'

The *Bulletin of the Lighter-than-Air Society*, issued in Akron, Ohio, in January, 1970, lists twenty-three Goodyear commercial non-rigid airships as having been built since 1928, three being in service at the date of publication. Of the latter, the *Mayflower* is 147,300 cubic feet; and the *America* and *Columbia* 202,700 cubic feet. A small replica of the French Lebaudy airship of 1903 was built in England in August 1967 for use in a film called Chitty Chitty Bang Bang, and was flown eleven times by Anthony Smith and Malcolm Brighton. It's volume was 43,000 cubic feet of helium.

There is an extremely interesting airship being completed by Harold Wingham, called the *Gloster*, at Cardington. The capacity is about 25,000 cubic feet of helium, and she is designed particularly for aerial photography work. No heavier-than-air craft, including helicopters with their excessive vibration, can equal the small airship for this requirement. Very considerable interest is being shown in the *Gloster* by the various bodies concerned in archaeology, for example.

Another airship of a very original character, designed and built by Mr Donald Cameron of Bristol and Dr. E.T. Hall of Oxford, is the first hot air airship ever to fly. A series of tests were made before construction was undertaken, for example with a water model filled upside down and a 20-foot long flying model. The first inflation of the full-sized airship took place on 1st November 1972 before any fins had been fitted, and a further flight after fitting a vertical fin in which some gentle S-turns were made. On 4th January 1973 the first real dirigible flight was achieved, and a public advertised flight was made at Newbury on the 7th January. Advantage was taken of the experience obtained on a previous attempt to fly Anthony Smith's *Wasp* about 1965; I myself had the honour of giving practical assistance during the development and early flights of the Cameron airship.

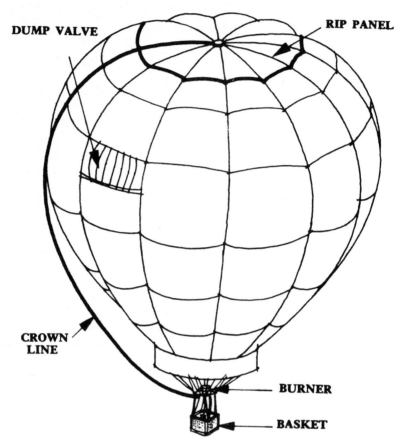

DUMP VALVE

RIP PANEL

CROWN
LINE

BURNER

BASKET

Diagram of a hot air balloon.

The hot air airship, of course, brings me back to the type of lighter-than-aircraft which was the forerunner of all flying: the free balloon lifted by hot air in 1783. Since this early date there have been many balloon flights, usually with coal gas or hydrogen as a lifting medium.

In the last few years, ballooning has taken on a new lease of life. In 1965 an international balloon race was held in England, in which ten hydrogen balloons from France, Germany, Holland, Belgium, Switzerland, the USA and Britain, took part. Recently there have been many notable flights, such as Anthony Smith's

Right: The first of the modern hot air balloons in England The *Bristol Belle* in 1967.

Below: T.B. Williams and Charles Dollfus in a balloon basket at Dunstable, April 1971.

journey across Africa; a trip over the Alps by Tom Sage and Gerry Turnbull; the crossings of the English Channel; the attempt to cross Australia; the flight over the Irish Sea by Ray Munro, a Canadian and the crossing of the Sahara, the latter by hot air balloons. We must also remember also the flights of Charles Dollfus, the Frenchman, who since 1911 has made over 500 ascents; and the further gallant attempt at crossing the Atlantic by Malcolm Brighton in September 1970.

A few years ago, hot air balloons were produced again, with the heat provided by propane, instead of burning straw and wool, as in the original Montgolfier.

In July 1966 the British Balloon and Airship Club was formed by several balloon enthusiasts and has grown considerably since the *Bristol Belle* was built at that time. Several keen hot air balloon clubs had been formed in various parts of the country. After meeting members of the Hot Air Group who were visiting Cornwall in June 1969, and finding a warm welcome as representing the Old Brigade, I was invited to join them at a ballooning week-end at Oxford in July, which I did and flew in several balloons again, the first time I had done so since my early World War I days and after a lapse of over fifty years — but this time the balloon was lifted by hot air instead of coal gas. We had six balloons up together, a wonderful sight with their different arrangements of colours. I flew in *Jester, Lumikon* and Balloon No.5, during the meeting and experienced a return of the earlier fascination of balloon flight. I have taken every opportunity for a flight since, in various parts of the country, usually with either Don Cameron or Tom Sage, two of the leading balloonists of the present time. As advertising in the air is now prohibited in this country some income is raised by demonstrations at sports meetings, agricultural shows and the like. This prohibition does not apply to Ireland, where recently a balloon had been sold to a group in Dublin.

Balloons are becoming more popular all the time. The *Wingfoot Bulletin* for February 1970 quotes some details of the Proceedings of the Fifth Scientific Balloon Symposium: a collection of 28

The crew of SR1 at Pulham in November 1918. T.B. Williams and Captain
George Meager are the two officers in the foreground.

At Greenham Common, Newbury, in July 1973. T.B. Williams is in the
centre, flanked by G.F. Meager and Lord Ventry.

papers which include: The Solar Powered Balloon; Flight Analysis of a Constant Level Expandable type Balloon; Conductive Balloon Material Study; Balloon Material Development; Inflight Deployment, a Unique Method for Launching Large Balloons; a Concept for an Extremely High Altitude Tethered Balloon System; and Performance Analysis and Selection of Balloon Electrical Power systems.

Balloons certainly will not lie down; after all they are lighter-than-air . . .

But what about the future of the great rigid airship, the liner of the air?

A good start to answering this question, I think, is given by W. Laurence Richards, an aeronautical development engineer. In an article in the *Sunday Times* of 8th January, 1967, written by W. Arthur Brenard, it is stated, under the heading '*We can build a safe fleet of airships now*':

> In a paper printed in the then current issue of *Tech Air*, the Journal of Licensed Aircraft Engineers and Technologists, W.L. Richards recalled that it was 30 years since the German *Hindenburg* caught fire and crashed at Lakehurst, New Jersey, which brought an end to the airship era.
>
> He believes that some of the shortcomings of the old airships are that they were not big enough, and sees the airships of the future as 1,000 feet long with a maximum diameter of 190 feet and a top speed of 115 to 120 miles per hour at 3,000 feet. Its gas would be non inflammable helium and a volume of 15,500,000 cubic feet; and nylon would be used as an outer skirt.
>
> Inside would be spacious cabins with luxurious accommodation for 400 passengers. Hot and cold showers would be provided — as was done in the Hindenburg.
>
> As a pure cargo carrier the airship would have a million cubic feet of cargo space and would be able to transport large power station transformers and enormous earth moving

machines direct from factories and deposit them on the sites where they were required.

W.L. Richards also suggests the possibility of air/sea rescue work, as an airship could hover over a stricken surface craft for days on end. In fact if the vessel was small, it could be lifted bodily out of the water or towed to safety.

Thom Keys who has produced a film called *Zeppelin* writes in an article printed in *Vogue* of July 1969 as follows:

The airship was an invention fifty years before its time. Atomic powered airships such as the one designed by Professor Francis Morse at the University of Boston mean perfect cruising with unlimited range. . . . The modern airship (and don't say we have not advanced in light new materials in the last thirty years) will have one million cubic feet of cargo space, will carry passengers in the luxury of a five star hotel. London to New York in forty uncramped hours. No airports – no runways – no noise – just moor at the heart of any city. Computerised courses, weather information from satellites, even though an airship will ride a storm better than any ship. Think! Plastics, helium, carbon fibres, atomic power. Factory to factory delivery of huge generators, on the site delivery of pipe lines, houses, raw material to roadless areas. No more loading for road, unloading at a port, re-loading for road to deliver abroad. For a nation which relies on her trade is it not a farce that the congested Port of London is worth more as real estate than as a port?
    Britain still smarts at the government botch-up of *R-101*. The private enterprise *R-100* was simply steam-rollered to save certain faces, and yet it was a brilliant ship designed by Sir Barnes Wallis, until recently head of research and development at the British Aircraft Corporation at the age of 82. A failing aircraft industry would do well to re-assess the future of the airship. . . . The airship is no monster, it is a phoenix. It should have its place in our vision of the future.

I have been in correspondence with Professor Morse and with the *New Scientist* who have printed details in their publication of 7th April 1966. I quote some of the details which are of immense importance. Professor Morse says the problems of adapting nuclear power to airships are fewer and less perplexing than those pertaining to the aeroplane. It is perfectly plain why. A primary consideration is weight: it has been estimated, for example, that in an aeroplane the size of the Super VC-10, of 335,000 pounds gross weight, fitted with a direct air cycle reactor containing lead and water shielding against radiation, the weight of the shielding alone would exceed 250,000 pounds. Obviously such an aeroplane would not take off, since the reactor weight exceeds its disposable lift. Increasing the size of the aircraft merely results in proportionately larger demands for power and also shielding.

An airship, which derives its lift from the buoyancy of helium, presents us with a very different set of figures. The power loading is actually only one fifteenth of that of the aeroplane, so that a large airship with a gross lift, say, of 760,000 pounds (2.3 times that of the Super VC-10) needs a power plant developing approximately 6,000 horsepower compared with over 40,000 horsepower for the airliner. The total weight of reactor and turbines, including shielding, will amount to some 120,000 pounds – substantially less than the weight of fuel alone which a conventionally powered airship of this size would need for a long journey.

A second serious obstacle confronting the designer of a nuclear aeroplane is the radiation hazard that an accident could produce. In a shattering impact with the ground, fissionable material might be spread over a wide area, with lamentable consequences. No one has even suggested a rational approach to this problem, which must be considered, however improbable a crash might be.

The problem is much less baffling with lighter than air craft. Intrinsic buoyancy reduces the inertial forces from an impact to a manageable level. The vast volume inside the hull provides the space needed for effective cushioning of the reactor. Its mass can be sprung so that it may shift position without rupturing either in the event of mid-air collision or impact with the ground. Obviously, this is the crucial subject as regards radiation safety.

Almost a score of letters appeared in the *Daily Telegraph* from March to May 1969 on airship revival. W. Peter Masefield led the attack; the defence being ably fought by Lord Ventry and Squadron Leader York-Moore. The best shot of all came from Professor J.D. Gillett who wrote:

Must we continue to have all this nonsense about airships? The trouble with those monsters of a bygone age was that they were before their time. Built of leaking bulls' guts and cotton, supported or not by an empirically designed frame of duralumin, wood or stainless steel, and the whole contraption filled with highly inflammable hydrogen, the amazing thing is that they achieved such notable success.

To be sure there were mishaps and accidents. They broke in half; they leaked and sank; they caught fire; yet, of the 600 or so airships, comparatively few crashed with loss of life. The case for the commercial airship has already been made; the record of the German passenger airships for reliability, comfort, and, yes, safety was remarkable.

It is worth noting that most of your correspondents who have so far written against the airships seem to be precisely those who know least about them. . . .

With an atomic power unit embedded in the inert lifting gas, situated hundreds of feet from passengers and crew and protected on all sides by the frame of the hull, the potentialities would be enormous.

On the 16th June, 1969, W.J.P.W. Mallalieu, Minister of State, Technology, 'with some nostalgic regret' in a written reply in the House of Commons to Raymond Fletcher, Labour MP for Ilkeston, refused a request that the Government should initiate a feasibility study of building nuclear powered airships. 'The commercial prospects do not justify public expenditure' he said. It sounds to me an echo of the Secretary of State for War who said

G

in 1910 that he could see no use for aircraft in war.

Much has already been learned in numerous experiments. Trials were carried out, for example, in lifting aeroplanes by airship in *R-23* and again in *R-33* when successful attachments and detachments were made in flight. The *Akron* had an internal aeroplane hangar and hooked on or detached aeroplanes in flight hundreds of times. With this ability, mails or passengers could be transferred in flight. As to handling, the high mooring masts at Cardington, Montreal and Lakehurst, and the experimental mast at Pulham, of which I was in charge up to the cessation of activities following he loss of *R-38*, proved the soundness of the system. On these masts airships have ridden out gales of 83 miles per hour.

The Americans have developed a method of mechanical handling with a transporter tower running on standard rail tracks to which the bow cone was attached; and the stern secured to a transverse beam, so that as the airship is towed out of the shed the stern can be brought round into the wind under control.

A water recovery system was also evolved which enabled water ballast to be condensed from the exhaust gases of the engines to the extent of approximately 100 pounds of water ballast for every 100 pounds of petrol burned and a system of scoops to catch rainwater. There were also experiments with refuelling airships from surface vessels at sea, but with nuclear power this need would disappear.

The Federal Aviation Commission of the United States summarized its findings on their airship losses, in these words:

> While the record of the airship has been marked by a number of disasters as a matter of common knowledge, each of them in turn has been the subject of detailed investigation and each appears to have shown, to the satisfaction of unprejudiced judges, to have been due either to errors in navigation or airmanship, which were in no way inevitable, or to a serious miscomprehension of the capacities of the airship. We find much in the record to indicate that the operation of airships is a highly specialized art, requiring long experience and the

highest order of skill. We cannot discover anything there that suggests any fundamental impossibility of safe and regular operation of large airships, or any lack of prospect of further improvement of the type.

We must remember the record of the *Graf Zeppelin* and the *Hindenburg*, the Goodyear blimps operating mostly away from hangars carried 400,000 passengers without harm; and there is the wonderful record of the British non-rigid fleet throughout the 1914-18 War.

As to comfort, Dr. Eckener once related how a number of very exhausted people came aboard the *Graf Zeppelin* in Brazil. The passengers had embarked after a long flight by aeroplane. Some 80 hours later they landed at Friedrichshafen feeling so well that some of them wished to remain on board. They looked upon the *Graf Zeppelin* as a pleasant convalescent home!

It must be remembered that since aeroplanes first took the air in 1903, well over a quarter of a million have been built and the most of the bugs have been knocked out of them, at a cost in lives of many thousands of passengers. Their success depends entirely on the excellence of the petrol or jet engine. No other means of transport depends so entirely on its motive power. No surface borne vessel or vehicle sinks at once if the means of propulsion fails, which facility is shared by the airship.

Only a few hundred airships have been built with the consequential limited experience. Thirteen passengers lost their lives, all on the *Hindenburg*, the only commercial passenger losses in the history of airships. As regards economy of operation, it should be sufficient to say that it requires 100 horsepower to move one ton of aeroplane and contents; but only 20 horsepower to move one ton of airship and contents. And, as for speed, already passengers crossing the Atlantic in fast jet propelled aeroplanes sometimes have to rest up on the other side often for days before they can attend to their business

What will happen when one leaves London after breakfast and reaches New York before breakfast?

An airship can bring you to your destination in comfort without sea sickness or exhaustion. There is a need for airships in the world, both large and small, to carry out work that no other vehicle can do as well. The revival is being continually suggested in some parts of the world, particularly the United States, Russia and Germany.

The *Sunday Times* of 26th July 1970 reported that pressure was being put on the Government to give the go-ahead to the development of a new generation of airships. Mr. Raymond Fletcher said the day before that members of both Houses of Parliament supported the plan.

> What we want [Mr. Fletcher said] are not airships in the old sense of the word. Using modern materials and technology, it is possible to produce craft which could carry 500 tons of containerised goods anywhere in the world, quickly, cheaply and safely.

> We believe that this idea — using the air like a railway system — is the answer to growing world trade and growing congestion on the existing means of transport.

During the last three months of 1970 there was considerable interest shown by many newspapers and technical publications, ranging as wide as *Flight International* to the *Financial Times*, in the prospect of airship revival, and there was an excellent broadcast on television by the BBC on 17th November. The culmination of all this was probably a full page article in the December issue of *Aerospace*, the monthly newspaper of the Royal Aeronautical Society, which had had articles and correspondence of the subject throughout the year. It gave some details of the objects of two companies formed to exploit the potentialities of airships for passenger and, particularly, cargo carrying. One is called Cargo Airships Limited — a subsidiary of Manchester Liners — and the other Airfloat Transport Limited. At least one other company has been floated with a particular interest in the transport of passengers and of motorcars. The airships have been already designed by Doctor Edwin Mowforth. In addition there is a very interesting project being worked on by Aerospace Developments for the Shell Companies, in which it is proposed to carry natural gas by airship. All the organisations have representatives as members of the Airship Association formed in 1971.

Shall I live to see the fulfilment? I don't know, but I am sure that it will come. In the meantime I have an invitation to attend an international balloon meeting, where I hope to get some more flights in the type of air vehicle that first flew in 1783: and I may be invited to fly again in *Europa* and with the Worlds first hot air airship designed by Don Cameron.

POSTSCRIPT

The end of the story takes me back to Anglesey and back some 50 years in time. In 1969 Flight Lieutenant W.N. Shuttleworth, who had been an airship pilot at Anglesey, presented the Anglesey County Council with a plaque in commemoration of the work carried out by the SS airships from the Royal Naval Airship Station at Bodffordd, Anglesey. It was presented 'on behalf of the Officers, Petty Officers and Ratings who served on the Airship Station during World War I and formed the RNAS Anglesey Old Boys' Association'. This 'Old Boys' Association' was formed soon after the end of the war and has held an annual reunion ever since. The first President was Captain E.L. Johnston, later the Navigating Officer of *R-101*; the second President was Major G.H. Scott, who was in charge of the last flight of *R-101*. Dinners were held every year during the period between the two World Wars, and again after World War II but were changed to luncheons during the years of the war. The Secretary throughout this whole period has been Chief Petty Officer H.J. Curtis, whose faithful service throughout fifty years has held the organisation together.

After the loss of *R-101* when both our original Presidents were killed, Captain G.L. Nicholls was appointed President, a position he held until he died in 1968, when I had the honour of being elected President in succession.

On Saturday, 6th December, 1969 our Association was invited

to attend the unveiling of the plaque which had been mounted in the entrance of the Shire Hall at Llangefni, Anglesey.

Unfortunately, Flight Lieutenant Shuttleworth had died a few weeks before the date of the unveiling, but had conveyed his wishes to Charles Morris Jones OBE, who had been at Anglesey and was an alderman in Bala, Merioneth; he made what arrangements were necessary. Ten representatives were able to attend the function, which was very impressive, followed by a luncheon given by Anglesey County Council at the Bull Hotel in Llangefni. Those attending included Captain George Meager, Lieutenant Warner and myself, with CPO Curtis — the Secretary — and six others.

In addition to most of the County Council being present, the Urban District Council was also strongly represented, the Press and Television cameras in attendance as well. We were honoured by the presence of the Commanding Officer of Valley, Holyhead, Royal Air Force Station, Group Captain W.E. Colahan. This Station, was now using our old landing ground, renamed Mona, for training.

On the 17th April 1970 the Association held the fiftieth and last organized gathering in London, as our numbers had become so few.

Bibliography

The Airship, a periodical edited by Lord Ventry and published between 1934 and 1948

Admiralty, Naval Air Service Training Manual 1915. Airship Service Monthly Items of Information. Handbooks on the various types of airships

Air Ministry, *Notes on Airships for Commercial Purposes*, 1918

Airship Guarantee Company *Airship R-100* Howden Yorkshire, Motor Books, 33 St Martins Court, London WC2

Aircraft Engineering January, February, June and November 1930. Articles on *R-100* by B.N. Wallis, P.L. Teed, and E.L. Johnston. Barnes Wallis was the chief designer, Teed was in charge of the gas and gas plant and Johnson was the navigation officer on the trans-atlantic flight. The latter was lost in the last flight of *R-101*

Ambers, Henry J., *The Dirigible and the Future*, Theo. Gaus' Sons, Inc. Brooklyn, N.Y. 11201

Andrews, C.F., *Vickers Aircraft since 1908*, Putnam, London, 1969

Barnes, C.H., *Shorts Aircraft since 1900*, Putnams, London, 1967

Barker, Ralph, *Aviator Extraordinary*, The Sidney Cotton Story, Newfoundland. Chatto and Windus, London, 1969

Boesman, Drs J. *Luchtschepen en Ballons*. Well illustrated. De Alkenreeks, Alkmaar, Holland

Botting, Douglas., *Shadow in the Clouds*, Radio Times 16th/22nd July 1966

Brewer, Griffiths, *Ballooning and Kite Ballooning*, Air League of the British Empire 1940

The Airship Association, *Phoenix Newsletters*, Secretary F.W. Hyde, 63 Cholmley Gardens, London N.W.6. Meetings at Caxton Hall, Victoria Street, London, S.W.1.

Brickhill, Paul, *The Dam Busters*, (Barnes Wallis and Air Chief Marshal the Hon. Sir Ralph Cochrane). Evans Bros. Ltd., London 1951

British Balloon and Airship Club, *Aerostat* Monthly Newsletters. *Free and Captive Balloons* and other publications. Artillery Mansions, 75 Victoria Street, London S.W.1

Brooks, Peter W., *Historic Airships*. (Good coloured plates and appendices.)

Broomfield, G.A., *Pioneer of the Air*, The Life & Times of S.F. Cody. Gale & Polden Ltd., Aldershot, 1953

Cave-Brown-Cave, J.R., *Safety from Fire in Airships*, R-38 Memorial Prize Lecture 1927, Royal Aeronautical Society, London.

Cameron, D.A., *Hot Air Balloon Operating Handbook*, Cameron Balloons Ltd., 1 Cotham Park, Bristol 6

Clarke, Basil, *The History of Airships*, Herbert Jenkins, London, 1961

Collier, Basil, *Leader of the Few*, The Dowding Story. Jarrolds, London, 1957

de Havilland, Sir Geoffrey, *Sky Fever*. Autobiography. Hamish Hamilton, London, 1961

Dollfus, Charles, *Balloons*, Prentice Hall International, London, 1962

Dudley, Ernest, *Monsters of the Purple Twilight*, The Life and Death of the Zeppelins. George G. Harrap & Co., Ltd. London, 1960

Duke, N. and Lanchbery, E., *The Crowded Sky*, An anthology. Cassell. London, 1959

Eckener, Hugo, *My Zeppelins*, Translated by D.H. Robinson. With a technical chapter by Knut Eckener. Putnam, London, 1958

Eiloart and Elstob, *The Flight of the Small World*, (Atlantic Ballooning). Hodder & Stoughton Ltd., London, 1959

Elliott, Christopher, *Aeronauts and Aviators*, (A history of early flying in the East Anglia area, including Pulham). Terence Dalton Ltd. Lavenham. Suffolk, 1971

Fisher, John, *Airlift 1870*, The balloons and pigeons in the Siege of Paris. Max Parrish, London, 1965

Fritsche, Carl B., *The Metalclad Airship*, Reprint of the Royal Aeronautical Society, London, 1931

Gibbs-Smith, C.H., *A Brief History of Flying*, Science Museum, London, 1967

Goodyear Tyre & Rubber Co. Ltd., *Aerial Ambassadors*, Goodyear Blimps. Akron, Ohio, U.S.A.

Grieder, Karl, *Zeppeline Giganten der Lüfte*. Well illustrated. Orell Fussli Verlag, Zurich, Switzerland

Gibbs-Smith, C.H., *The Aeroplane*, An Historical Survey. Science Museum, London, 1960

Gibbs-Smith, C.H. and Oliver Warner, *Balloons and Ships*, 19th Century Coloured Prints. K.G. Lohse, Graphischer, Frankfurt am Main, Germany

Higham, Robin, *The British Rigid Airship 1908-31*, G.J. Foulis & Co. Ltd., London, 1968

Hogg, Garry, *Airship over the Pole*, The story of the Italia. Abelard-Schuman Ltd., London, 1969

Horton, Edward, *The Age of the Airship*, Sidgwick & Jackson Ltd., London, 1973

Hurren, B.J., *Fellowship of the Air*, The Jubilee Book of the Royal Aero Club 1901-1951. Published for 'Flight' by Iliffee & Sons Ltd., 1951

Jackson, Robert, *Airships in Peace and War*, (includes details of the 'Aereon' airship and a good Chronology). Cassell, London, 1971

Keller, C.L., *U.S.S. Shenandoah*, World War One Aero Publishers, Inc. West Roxbury, Mass. 02132, U.S.A. 1964

Keys, Thom., *The Zeppelin Legend*, Vogue Magazine, London, July 1969

Kirschner, E.J., *The Zeppelin in the Atomic Age*, University of Illinois, U.S.A. 1957

Leasor, James, *The Millionth Chance*, (The story of R-101). Hamish Hamilton, London, 1957

Lipper, Harold W., *Helium Symposia Proceedings*, Bureau of Mines 1969. United States Department of the Interior

Lighter-Than-Air-Society, The, 1800 Triplett Blvd., Akron, Ohio 44306, United States of America

Litchfield, P.W. and Allen, Hugh, *Why has America no Rigid Airship?* Corday & Cross Co., Cleveland, Ohio, 1945

Lufthansa International, *We'll do what we can*, Lufthansa International, London, 1969

Lucke, Charles E., *Aircraft of Belligerents in the year 1914*, (Volume 2: Airships) U.S. Navy Gas Engine School. Translated from the German. Publisher: Flying Enterprises Mitchen Mayborn 3209 Coral Rock Lane, Dallas, Texas, 75229, 1971

Masters, David, *Up Periscope*, Eyre and Spottiswoode, London, 1943

McKinty, Alec, *The Father of British Airships*, A Biography of E.T. Willows. William Kimber and Co. Ltd., London, 1972

Meager, George, *My Airship Flights*, William Kimber and Co. Ltd., London, 1970

Mooney, Michael M., *The 'Hindenburg'*, Hart-Davis, MacGibbon, London, 1973

Morpurgo, J.E., *Barnes Wallis*, (including the story of R-80 and R-101). Longman, London, 1972

Morris, Alan, *The Balloonatics*, (Kite-Balloons in action). Jarrolds, London, 1970

Morse, Francis, *The Nuclear Airship*, (The design of a professor of Boston University, U.S.A.) New Scientist Magazine, 7th April, 1966

Nielsen, Thor, *The Zeppelin Story*, The Life of Hugo Eckener. Allan Wingate, London, 1955

Nowarra, Robertson and Cooksley, *Marine Aircraft of the 1914-1918 War*, (including airships and engines), Harleyford Publications Ltd., Letchford, Hertfordshire, 1966

Nobile, Umberto, *My Polar Flights,* Frederick Muller Ltd., London 1961

Penrose, Harold, *British Aviation: The Great War and Armistice 1915-1919*, Putnam, London, 1969

Picard, Auguste, *Between Earth and Sky*, Translated from the French by Claude Archer. Balloon flying in the stratosphere. Falcon Press (London) Limited, 1950.

Price, A. *Aircraft versus Submarine'*, William Kimber, London, 1973. The evolution of the anti-submarine aircraft, including airships, 1972

Popham, Hugh, *Into Wind* A History of Naval Flying including airships. Hamish Hamilton, London, 1967

Pudney, John, *The Camel Fighter,* Hamish Hamilton, London 1964

Richards, L.P. *We can build a safe fleet of airships,* Sunday Express 6th January 1967

Robinson, Douglas H., *Giants in the Sky,* A History of the rigid airship. G.T. Foulis & Co., Ltd., Henley-on-Thames, Oxfordshire, 1973. A very useful book.

Robinson, Douglas H., *LZ 129 Hindenburg,* Morgan-Dallas. Arco-New York, U.S.A.

Rolt, L.T.C. *The Aeronauts,* A history of ballooning 1783-1903. Longmans Green & Co., Ltd., 1966

Royal Aero Club, Year Books

Royal Aeronautical Society, *Aerospace,* Monthly Newspapers

Royal Engineers, *Military Ballooning 1862,* A reprint of three papers read at Chatham in that year. Aviation Press, 150 Broadfields Avenue, Edgware, Middlesex, 1967

Saundby, Sir Robert, *Early Aviation,* Library of the 20th C. Macdonald, London, 1971. American Heritage Press, New York 10017

Saunders, Hilary St. George, *Per Ardua,* The Rise of British Air Power 1911-1939. Oxford University Press, 1944

Santos-Dumont, A. *My Airships,* Grant Richards, London, 1904

Scott, G.H. *Handling and Mooring of Airships,* (R-38 Memorial Lecture 1929). Royal Aeronautical Society, London

Shell Aviation News, *The Gentle Art of Blimping* by Harold Wingham. *The Small World of Mr Wu* by Air Marshal Sir Victor Goddard. Issue 331 and 254,

Shute, Nevil, *Slide Rule* (R-100). William Heinemann Ltd., London, 1954.

Simmons, George, *Target: Arctic,* Men in the Skies at the top of the World. Chilton Books, Philadelphia: New York, 1965

Sinclair, J.A. *Airships in Peace and War,* Rich and Cowan Ltd., London, 1934

Sinclair, J.A. *Famous Airships of the World,* Frederick Muller Ltd., London, 1959

Smith, Anthony, *Throw Out Two Hads,* Across Africa by George Allen & Unwin, London, 1963 balloon

Smith, Anthony, *The First Five Years of the British Balloon and Airship Club,* B.B.A.C. Artillery Mansions, 75 Victoria Street, London S.W.1

Smith, Anthony, *Throw Out Two Hands.* Balloon Across Africa by George Allen & Unwin, London, 1963.

Sprigg, C. St. John, *Great Flights,* Thomas Nelson & Sons Ltd., London, 1935

Sprigg, T. Stanhope, *The Aero Manual 1910,* Reproduced in 1972 by David & Charles, Publishers Ltd., Newton Abbot, Devon

Toland, John, *Ships in the Sky,* Frederick Muller Ltd., London, 1957. (Reprinted in 1972 by Dover Publications Inc., New York, under the title 'The Great Dirigibles'.)

Turnbull, Christine, *Hot Air Ballooning,* Speed and Sports Publications Ltd., Acorn House, Victoria Road, Acton, London, W.3, 1970

Vaeth, J. Gordon, *Graf Zeppelin*, The Adventures of an Aerial Globetrotter. Harper & Brothers, New York, U.S.A.

Villard, Henry Serrano, *Contact*, The Story of the Early Birds. Arthur Barker Limited, 5 Winsley Street, London W.1, 1968

Walker, Percy B., *Early Aviation at Farnborough*, Volume I; Balloons, Kites & Airships. Macdonald, London, 1971

Ward, Charles E. and P. de L. Dyson-Skinner, *Who's Who in British Aviation*, Bunhill Publications, 112 Bunhill Row, London E.C.1, 1935 and 1936

Whale, George, *British Airships: Past Present and Future*, John Lane, The Bodley Head, London and New York, 1919

Whitehouse, Arch, *The Zeppelin Fighters*, Robert Hale Limited, 1966

Williams, T.B., *Airship Mooring in England*, 'The Airship' Magazine, 1937/9

Wykes, Alan, *Air Atlantic*, A History of Transatlantic Flying. Hamish Hamilton, London, 1967

Yeatman, Jonathan, *Daffodil and Golden Eagle*, (The saga of two balloons crossing the Sahara). Aidan Ellis Publishing Ltd., Henley-on-Thames, 1972

Young, Edward, *One of our Submarines*, (Possibly one of the best books published after the Second World War on submarine warfare) 1952. Originally published by Hart-Davis. Paperback by Penguin in 1954. Revised paperback by Pan in 1968

Gray, Edwin, *A Damned Un-English Weapon*, Submarine Warefare in the First World War, with appendices of British Submarines 1900-1918. Seeley, Service & Co., London, 1971

Shankland, Peter and Hunter, Anthony, *Dardanelles Patrol*, The Incredible Story of the E.11 under the command of (now) Admiral Sir Martin Dunbar-Nasmith, V.C. William Collins, 1964, London.
Both the above books have been published in paperbacks: the first by the New English Library and the second by Mayfair Books: 1973 and 1971 respectively.

Lee, Arthur Gould, *No Parachute* With an interesting Appendix C dealing with 'why no parachutes' in World War One. Jarrolds Publishers (London) Ltd., 1968, also published in paperbacks by Arrow Books 1969

Williamson, Cathy, *Falling Free*, Robert Hale, London, 1965
An autobiographic account written by a young parachuting instructress.

Payne, Air Commodore L.G.S., *Air Dates*, A chronological survey of the principle events in the fields of military and civil aviation in Great Britain and abroad, beginning in 1783 with balloon ascents in Paris, and ending on 31st December 1956.

(Reprinted from *The Airship*)
BRITISH SERVICE AIRSHIP STATISTICS 1914-1918

1914-1918
Airships built or used:

Non Rigids	207
Semi Rigid	1
Rigids	8
	216

Approx. number of each class:
SS 49. SSP. 6. SSZ. 75. SST. 14
S.S. ships of all types, 144

Coastals, 32
Coastal Stars, 10
North Seas, 18
Parseval, 3
R9, 1
R23 class, 4 (R23, 24, 25, 26)
R23X class, 2. (R27, R29)
R31 class, 1

Hours Flown (Naval Airships) 1912-1918

1912/1913		
1914/1915	about	3,250
1916		7,078
1917		22,389
1918		56,000

88,717 hours = 10 years
Mooring-Out Sites: 12; 237,360 miles flown from these.

Operational Statistics, 1917 and 1918
June 1917-Oct 1918 (when non-rigid stations were all manned)

Airships	56
Patrols	9,059
Escorts	2,216
Miles	1,496,006
Hours	59,704
Flights approx.	10,150
Airships Lost	16
U boats sighted	49
Mines sighted	134

Table showing increasing use of Airships

1918	Jan.	Feb.	Mar.
No. of Patrols	174	268	602
No. of Escorts	47	37	132
Duration (hours)	832	1416	4054
Flying Hrs. man employed	.26	.44	1.24

Airships stations, 1918

United Kingdom (Ops.)	9
Abroad (Ops.)	1
U.K. Erectional	5
U.K. Training	1
U.K. Experimental	1
	17

Best Endurances

SST.14	52 hrs. (Capt. G.F. Meager, A.F.C.)
SSZ.39	56 hrs. 55 mins. (Capt. Bryan, A.F.C.)
C.24	24 hrs. 15 mins.
C*.	34 hrs. 10 mins. (Capt. Cleary)
NS.11	100 hrs. 50 mins. (Capt. W. Warneford, A.F.C.)
B26 Rigid	(Op flight) 40 hrs. 40 mins. (Major T. Elmsley)

Details of losses (approx.)
Airships lost:

At Sea	15
Enemy action	2 (C.17, C27)
Burnt in Sheds	10
Burnt in Air	2 (NS.11, SST.6)
Destroyed on landing ground	3
Miscellaneous	8
	40

Lives lost: 48 from all causes.
Miles flown per loss of life: 46,787 miles.

Ships in use (approx.)

1914 (Aug.)	5	Constructed	213
1915 (Jan.)	5	Reconstructed	13
1916 (Jan.)	22	Transferred to Allies	23
1917 (Jan.)	58	Deleted	100
1918 (Nov.)	103	In commission Nov. 1918	103

Rigid Airships
No

1. Broke up leaving shed, 1911
9. Deleted, 1918 (out of date)
23.⎤ Deleted, 1918/19 (out of date). R.24 and 26 were used
24.⎟ for mooring mast experiments.
25.⎟
26.⎦
27. Burnt in shed, 1918. (Howden, due to fire started in SS. Zero).
29. Deleted, 1920, out of date.
31. Deleted as dangerous owing to wood rotting, 1919.
32. Deleted, 1921, on shutting down of R.A.F. Airship Service.
33. Deleted, 1927 (still in flying order. Economy.)
34. Broke up on landing ground, 1921, (due entirely to lack of mooring mast).

36. Deleted, 1927 (economy).
38. Crashed and lost, 1921. (Ship known to be weak. Trials rushed due to closing down of Airship Service.)
80. Deleted 1927. Economy.
100. Deleted, 1930. (Economy, sold for £450!)
101. Crashed and lost, 1930. (Trials hurried for ship to fly to India on an arranged date.)

Army Airships, 1907-1914
Nulli Secondus I, 1907
Nulli Secondus II, 1908. (Reconstructed Alpha.)
Baby, 1909.
Beta I, 1910. Reconstructed Baby. Deleted 1914 out of date.
Beta II, 1912 (new and larger ship) deleted 1916 out of date.
Gamma, 1910-1914. Deleted 1914 (enlarged 1912) out of date.
Delta, 1912-1916. Deleted 1916, out of date.
Eta I, 1913-1914. Wrecked while moored, Nov. 20th 1914 on way to Belgium.
*Eta II, 1916. (Spare Eta envelope & French car. Deleted 1916 too slow.)
Army operational flights about 10; including 4 over lines in France, SS.40 in 1916.
* On Jan. 1st 1914 the existing Military Airships were handed over to the Naval Wing, R.F.C.

Beta II became Naval airship	17	
Gamma	18	January 1914
Delta	19	
Eta	20	

Appendix 2
Comparative sizes of some Airships

BRITISH	Capacity cubic feet in thousands.	Length in feet	Beam in feet
Non-rigid			
SS1	24		
SS (BE2c and MF)	60	143	27
SS (A.W., Pusher & Zero)	70	143	30
SS Twin	100	164	32
Coastal	170	194	39
Coastal Star	210	218	49
North Sea	360	262	58
Semi Rigid: (SR 1)	441	269	59
Rigid			
R1	663	512	48
R9	890	526	53
R23 class	1000	535	53
R31 class	1500	615	60
R33 class	2000	643	79
R36 class	2750	695	85
R80	1250	535	70
R100	5000	709	133
R101	5500	725	133

United States of America

Non Rigid Type:	cu. ft. in thousands	Length in feet	Beam in feet
A	110	175	35
B	77	156	34
C	180	192	43
D	190	198	43
E	95	150	30
F	95	160	31
G	178	184	44
K	416	248	57
L	123	147	37

Rigids			
Shenandoah	2105	680	79
Los Angeles	2470	656	91
Akron	6850	785	133
Macon	6850	785	133

German (Rigid)			
L1 Naval Zeppelin	776	525	50
Graf Zeppelin	4000	775	100
Hindenberg	7000	813	135

The expression of capacity of so many cubic feet can be considered in tons gross buoyancy.

One million cubic feet equals 30 tons approximately.

Five million cubic feet equals 150 tons approximately.

Thus R101 with gas bags, framework, engines, etc., came to a gross weight of 100 tons and there was left 50 tons which could be used for useful purposes to carry petrol, passengers, mails, etc.

Built in 1918 at Ciampino, Rome.

Capacity	441,000 cubic feet
Ballonets	200,000 cubic feet
Length	269 feet
Width	59 feet
Overall height	87 feet

Weights:

Envelope, planes and tanks	10,575 lbs.
Car, engines, wireless etc.	8,000 lbs.
Disposable	6,800 lbs.
Crew of nine	1,400 lbs.

Engines:
Two Itala-Maybach, One S.P.A.
each a nominal 200-220 h.p.
Speed about 50 miles per hour.

Other Italian Semi-Rigids
A type of a million cubic feet approximately.
O type a little larger than our S.S.

Appendix 4
Specification of S.S.Z. non-rigid airship

Volume 70,000 cubic feet
Ballonet capacity, each of two, 9,800 cubic feet
Beam 30 feet
Overall height 44 feet 6 inches
Length of car, from stem to locknut of propeller boss 18' 6"
Diameter of four-bladed propeller 7 feet 10 inches
Area of plane surfaces, two elevators and two flaps, rudder plane
 and rudder, 517,5 square feet
Height obtained by ballonets, 8,400 feet
Estimated increase of volume by stretch of envelope, 2,000 to
 3,000 cubic feet
Petrol tanks, two, capacity of both 102 gallons
Oil tank, 4½ gallons
Water ballast bag capacity, 28 gallons (280 lbs)
Engine: Rolls-Royce Hawk, 75 h.p.
Speed and consumption:
 Theoretical endurance of 16 hours at 1,300 revolutions = 56
  miles per hour at a petrol consumption of 6.5 gallons per
  hour
 Theoretical endurance of 40 hours at 700 revolutions = 20 miles
  per hour at a petrol consumption of 2.5 gallons per hour
Climb: maximum angle at full speed 43°
Maximum speed 1,200 feet per minute
Volume of gas lost per 1,000 feet rise = 2,300 c. feet
Descent: maximum angle at full speed 51°
maximum speed of descent 1,400 feet per minute.
Turning circle at full speed 40 seconds either way
Diameter of circle 700 feet; circumference 2,200 feet. Above in
 still air.

S.S. Zero Airship: Weights and Lifts

	lbs.
Envelope with all fittings	1530
Planes, flaps and rudder	307
Rigging and metal fittings	140
	1977
Engine, propeller and tanks	498
Armament and wireless	230
Car frame, covering and seats	451
	3156
Disposable load:	
Crew of three	450
Petrol 60 gallons	420
Oil 4 gallons	36
Radiator water	40
Grapnel, tailrope, drogue, lifebelts Very pistol etcetera	105
Bombs	130
Water ballast	163
Lift of gas at 95% purity	4500

Appendix 5
Comparative characteristics of a proposed Nuclear Airship and the Hindenburg.

	Nuclear Airship	Hindenburg
Overall length, feet	980	803
Maximum diameter, feet	172	135
Fineness ratio, L/D	5.70:1	5.95:1
Maximum gas volume, cubic feet	12.5 million	7.2
Lifting gas	Helium	Hydrogen
Gross lift, at 95% inflation, lbs.	760,000	455,000
Useful lift, lbs.	300,000	230,000
Payload, lbs.	180,000	40,000
Number of passengers	400	72
Number of personnel	95	54
Number of gas cells	17	16
Number of engines	3	4
Total horsepower	6,000	4,800
Maximum speed, miles per hour	103	85.6
Cruising speed, miles per hour	95	78
Range, statute miles	Unlimited	8000

The nuclear airship is the design of Professor Francis Morse of the University of Boston U.S.A.

ACKNOWLEDGEMENTS

Photographs & Diagrams

p. 40, reproduced by permission of the British Standards Institution, 2 Park Street London from an obsolete edition of BS 185, Aeronautical glossary; p. 48, Imperial War Museum; pp. 56-7, and 66, Royal Aeronautical Society; p. 96, Public Record Office, ERB 40; p. 105, Royal Aeronautical Society; p. 117, Imperial War Museum; p. 138, Imperial War Museum; p. 158, Imperial War Museum; p. 164, National Archives, Washington DC; p. 168, Imperial War Museum; p. 179, Harold Wingham; p. 184, West Deutsche Luftwerbung; p. 184, *Goodyear Europa* by Tom Sage; p. 184, *Hotair Airship* by Tom Sage; p. 187, Press Association; p. 189, Goodyear Tyre & Rubber Company.

Quotations in the text

p. 23, *My Airships*, Alberto Santos-Dumont, Grant Richards 1904; p. 28, *Sky Fever*, Sir Geoffrey de Haviland, Hamish Hamilton, London, 1961; p. 46, *Airmen or Noahs*, Rear Admiral Murray Sueter, Pitman, London, 1928; p. 58, *Camel Fighter*, John Pudney, Hamish Hamilton, London, 1964; p. 86, *Mr Wu*, Air Marshal Sir Victor Goddard, Shell Aviation News No. 254; p. 102, *The Dam Busters*, Paul Brickhill, Evans Brothers, London, 1951; p. 134, *Aviator Extraordinary*, The Sidney Cotton Story as told to Ralph Barker, Chatto & Windus, London, 1969; p., 148, *The British Rigid Airship, 1908-1931*, Robin Higham, G.T. Foules, London, 1961; p. 156, *Slide Rule*, Nevil Shute, William Heinemann, London, 1954; p. 159, *My Airship Flights*, Captain George Meager, William Kimber, London, 1970; p. 165, *The*

Millionth Chance, James Leasor, Hamish Hamilton, London, 1967; p. 165, *Sunday Dispatch* of 19th March, 1933; p. 175, *Famous Airships of the World*, J.A. Sinclair, Frederick Muller, London, 1959; p. 175, *The Radio Times* of 18th July 1966; p. 176, Lufthansa International: *We'll do all we can;*; p. 177, *The Gentle Art of Blimping* by Harold Wingham, Shell Aviation News No. 331; p. 190, *Sunday Times* of 8th January 1967; p. 191, *Zeppelin Legend* by Thom Keys, Vogue Magazine of July 1969; p. 192 and Appendix No.5: *The Nuclear Airship*, Professor Morse of Boston University 'New Scientist' of 7th April 1966; p. 194, Findings of the Federal Aviation Committee of the United States of America; Appendix No.1, Lord Ventry for statistics from 'The Airship'.

A last word of thanks to Elizabeth Swann, who did most of the typing, and to Ronald Doyle who dealt so expertly with some of the photographs.

Index

Names of airships are listed
under the sub-heading — Airships